Sutter's

OWN STORY

The Life of
General John Augustus Sutter
and the History of New Helvetia
in the Sacramento Valley

ILLUSTRATED

By

ERWIN G. GUDDE

G · P· PUTNAM'S SONS
New York
1936

PRINTED IN
THE UNITED STATES OF AMERICA
Van Rees Press
NEW YORK

Sutter's Own Story

I doubt if a more remarkable instance of indi- vidual energy, perseverance and heroism, has ever been displayed under similar circumstances. This unceremonious way of settling down in a strange country, and founding a sort of independent em- pire on 'one's own hook', is one of those feats which will excite the astonishment of posterity. In times past, men have been deified on slighter grounds.

JOSEPH W. REVERE, 1849.

JOHN AUGUSTUS SUTTER

Painting by Frank Buchser in the
Museum of the City of Solothurn

Contents

[v]

Illustrations

[vii]

Maps

Sutter's Own Story

I

The Years in Europe

THE men of Seldwyla are unlike those of other
Swiss towns, if we believe what Gottfried Keller,
the Swiss poet, tells us about them in his charming
stories. When they reach the middle of their thir-
ties, the age in which men of other communities
begin to amount to something, they are played out
and done for. The majority of them stay right in
town, occupied with all sorts of trifling and boot-
less enterprises. But those few who can pluck up
enough courage pack their bundles and seek their
fortune in the wide world. One can find natives of
Seldwyla in Paris and in Constantinople as well as

[1]

in Australia, in Texas, and in California, and some of them have made good names for themselves after leaving the sunny valley in which they could not thrive.

Such a man was Johann August Sutter; and who can stand up and say that the poet did not think of the great pioneer when he wrote the preface to his imaginary *Seldwyla Folks* in 1856?

Sutter was the scion of an old Alemanic family whose name was usually spelled Suter, and sometimes Souter. The grandfather of our hero, Johann Jakob, left his native village Rünenberg, learned the trade of a papermaker in old, venerable Basel and settled finally in Kandern, within the territory belonging to the Margrave of Baden. This little Black Forest town, whose surrounding landscape bears a certain resemblance to the foothills of the Sierra Nevada, was to be the home of the Sutter family for several generations although they retained their citizenship in Rünenberg. Here the Swiss emigrant worked his way up to the position of *Papiermeister*, a foreman or manager of the papermill. His son, born on the second of January,

1776, and named likewise Johann Jakob, followed in his father's footsteps and became in due time his successor. In 1801 he was married to Christina Wilhelmina Stöber, a pastor's daughter from the frontier village of Grenzach. Their first child, either born or baptized on February the twenty-third, 1803, was our Johann August. Two other boys, the twin brothers Johann Heinrich and Jakob Friedrich, were born five years later.

Until his sixteenth year, the papermaker's son attended the schools of his native town and was then, apparently only for a short time, a pupil at St. Blaise near Neuchâtel. In 1819 we find him as an apprentice to the publisher and bookseller, Emanuel Thurneysen, in the city of Basel—his insatiable desire for reading may have influenced this choice. However, he was not destined to be a dealer of books: between 1822 and 1828 he clerked, first for a cloth merchant in Aarburg, then for a grocer in Burgdorf. The window panes in Switzerland are obviously not as easily broken as in the United States: a little yellowed lattice in the storeroom of the former grocery of Aeschlimann still bears Sutter's name, scratched with the diamond of his ring.

Sutter's career in the little town of Burgdorf, his Seldwyla, forms the prelude to his short but brilliant appearance on the stage of history. The first documentary evidence of his presence there we find in the record of his marriage to Anna Dübeld, the daughter of a well-to-do widow, who was carrying on the bakery and restaurant of her late husband. In consequence of this somewhat precipitate act, which took place on the twenty-fourth of October, 1826, he found it necessary to establish himself in business. On the twenty-sixth of August, 1828, he bought from the widow Trechsel-Grimm a house on Schmieden-Alley, which burned down thirty-seven years later, by a strange coincidence within a fortnight of the conflagration at Hock-Farm. In this house he established a cloth and yarn business. The publishing house conducted in partnership with his former co-apprentice, J. J. Weber, the founder of the world-renowned publishing business in Leipzig, was a figment of Sutter's fertile imagination in later years, as were his commission in the Swiss army and his acquaintance with Napoleon III.

Within a few years Sutter came to the sad realization that as a merchant he was a decided failure. To be sure, the insolvency of Sutter and Company may have been hastened by his profligate partner and by the distrust which the Bernese people felt for the enterprising "foreigner." But the chief cause for his failure lay certainly in the same peculiarities of his mental make-up, which in later years brought about the downfall of his California empire: his almost pathological desire to live and to conduct business in grand style, his readiness to contract debts and to make promises, his princely open-handed liberality, his utter inability to calculate and to attend to the details of business. As early as May 1832, he was obliged to sell the house to his mother-in-law, and two years later Switzerland became too small for Johann August. Toward the end of May 1834, he left wife and children and embarked at Havre for the United States. The warrant of arrest which followed him under date of June the twelfth, cast a stain upon him which he could never entirely obliterate. Yet, there was little else that could have been done. A term in the debtor's prison would neither have helped his family, nor enabled him to repay the good round sum of thirty-five thousand francs, by which his liabilities exceeded his assets. His flight, on the other hand, gave him the opportunity to build up a new existence and to satisfy his debtors —though his last obligations were not met until some twenty years afterwards. And Anna Dübeld Sutter showed that admirable courage and prowess which women are apt to develop under such circumstances. When she rejoined her husband fifteen years later on the banks of the Feather River, she could present to him with pride four well-educated young people, three sons and one daughter.

II

Over Land and Sea to Yerba Buena

THE final conquest by the United States of the vast territories between the Rocky Mountains and the Pacific Ocean became a historical necessity after the Louisiana Purchase had removed the most important obstacle in the way of the westward movement of the young nation. How soon the great human wave would reach the shores of the ocean, however, no one could foretell in the fourth decade of the nineteenth century. Lands for settlement were cheap and plentiful in the fertile plains east and west of the Mississippi, while the barren stretches beyond the boundaries of the old French territory offered little or no inducements. California itself—whose sudden fame was to bring about a consolidation of the continent only a few years later—was little more than a geographical conception. Since Alexander von Humboldt had published his report on the *Provincia de la Nueva California,* a number of American and German, English and French authors had written about this territory from personal observation, and occasionally returning trappers and traders would start a tale among the people about the land of perpetual sunshine and hospitable inhabitants. The three hundred odd Yankees and Europeans who had more or less accidentally remained in California usually married dark-haired *señoritas* and were absorbed by the native element. California was waiting for the man who would place her name on the map and push the clock of time a few decades ahead. And this man was destined to be no other than the bankrupt German-Swiss yarn dealer—Johann August Sutter.

Here starts Sutter's own story.

'In July 1834, I landed in New York. My object

'in coming to America was to become a farmer.
'With a few friends, two Germans and two French-
'men, I traveled through Indiana and Ohio. We
'agreed not to learn English as long as we were to-
'gether. However, after a while we parted, and I
'went to Missouri.

'The winter of 1834-35 I spent in St. Louis and
'St. Charles. I had brought with me from Switzer-
'land some means, with which I purchased a piece
'of land in Missouri. But I did not like the country.
'It was too cold in the winter, the district was still
'sparsely settled, and there seemed to be no market
'for agricultural products. Missouri was at that
'time still the Indian frontier. When I became ac-
'quainted with Sante Fe traders I made up my
'mind to go with a trading company to this Mexi-
'can business center. On my way to Santa Fe I met
'at Taos Mr. Popian, the *alcalde* of this city. Mr.
'Popian was an educated Canadian, who had stud-
'ied for the clergy but had never taken the orders.
'This gentleman had been in the southern part of
'California and gave me much information about
'this country. He said that it was a beautiful re-

'gion with a fine climate and perpetual summer.

'So I sold out and decided to try my luck in California.'

No great success seems to have attended Sutter's enterprise in Santa Fe, where, by the way, another member of the Swiss Sutter clan, one Pedro Soutter, had lived as early as 1749. A group of Germans, whom Johann August with his never failing enthusiasm had induced to invest time and money in his ventures, used no flattering words in telling of his business methods. This imputation of unfair transactions by his disappointed partners may have had something to do with his relinquishing the idea of farming in Missouri or trading in New Mexico in favor of the more ambitious scheme of becoming a pioneer in California. The cash at his disposal was probably very limited, but in his indefatigable optimism and his magnetic personality he possessed a valuable capital which was to stand him in good stead.

Three routes to California were possible: the overland route through Utah, the track over which in later years the caravans of emigrants traveled;

the Oregon trail via Fort Hall, a trading post established a few years ago by the doughty Nathaniel Wyeth; and the old Spanish trail by which many of the older pioneers such as Leese, Wolfskill, and Yount had reached the Pueblo de los Angeles. The idea of going by the direct course was not seriously considered. Only two parties, Jedediah Smith's in 1827, and Captain Joseph Walker's in 1833, had succeeded in reaching the coast across the central Sierras, escaping the dangers of the desert and the arrows of the Indians. Sutter had almost decided to take the southern route when one of his friends convinced him that the way over Fort Hall and Fort Vancouver was the better one. It turned out to be poor advice, for it delayed Sutter's arrival in the promised land by almost a year.

'My first intention had been to go to California 'via Sonora. But Sir William Drummond Stewart, 'a Scotchman, advised me to take the route over 'Fort Hall, a station of the Hudson's Bay Com-'pany on the road to Oregon. Stewart had been 'buffalo hunting several times in the Rocky Moun-

'tains, though he had never crossed them. He told
'me that this route was shorter and easier, and that
'at Fort Hall I should be able to find men who
'would be willing to accompany me to California.
'On account of the war-like Indians, I could not
'think of going directly to California.

'I engaged six men, all experienced mountain-
'eers, and a Mexican servant; three of my men were
'Germans, two Yankees, and one was a Belgian.
'We started on our overland journey to California
'on April eleventh, 1838. To the Rendezvous in the
'Wind-River-Valley we traveled in company of a
'party of the American Fur Company under Cap-
'tain Tripps. Before we reached this place we en-
'countered many dangers from the Indians. At that
'time, the Rendezvous consisted of a few block
'houses and stores where hunters and trappers
'bought their supplies. Every year the traders and
'trappers would meet here for a few weeks to make
'their barters. It was only a temporary trading
'post. I could find enough men here to accompany
'me to California, but I was wise enough not to
'accept them. They wanted to organize as a band

'of robbers under my leadership in order to steal
'cattle and rob missions and settlements.

'The commander at Fort Hall, a Swiss by the
'name of Franz Ermatinger, gave me an Indian
'guide. The Indians were at that time not very
'friendly toward Americans and it was necessary
'for my compatriot to tell them that I was a "King
'George Man" and not a "Boston." This guide con-
'ducted me through the Indian territory to Fort
'Boise, the same spot where Boise City now stands.

'At Fort Boise I was received in a very friendly
'manner by the commander, Payette, a French Ca-
'nadian. How glad we were to come to a resting
'place where we could get something decent to eat!
'There I got another guide to conduct me to Fort
'Walla Walla where the commander, Tambrun,
'likewise received me very kindly. He was an edu-
'cated man who had served as an officer in the Brit-
'ish Army. Since I was not accustomed to horse
'meat, it struck me as quite singular when the com-
'mander said at our departure: "I am sorry you
'are going now, I have just killed a fat mare."

'After resting a few days at Walla Walla, I pro-

'cured a new guide to bring us to The Dalles, at the
'rapids of the Columbia River. The Dalles was a
'model settlement for that early date, combining a
'Methodist mission with a trading establishment,
'both in charge of H. K. W. Perkins and Daniel
'Lee. When I asked for a guide to the Willamette
'Valley, Mr. Lee told me that he himself would
'bring me there. He intended to exchange horses,
'which he had purchased from the Indians, for
'cattle in the Willamette Valley.

'The first day out my mountaineers were greatly
'dissatisfied with the course pursued by Mr. Lee.
' "How he lies!" they exclaimed.

' "Lies?" said I. "Why, he does not say anything
'at all!"

' "Nevertheless, he is lying," they said, "see how
'he twists and turns about. At this rate he will
'bring us back to our starting point."

'So impatient did they become of the circuitous
'route of Mr. Lee that they rebelled and insisted on
'taking a more direct course. As I myself was anx-
'ious to reach California before the end of the year,
'I finally gave in. So we struck out over the moun-

SUTTER'S BIRTHPLACE IN KANDERN

YERBA BUENA

'tains through the wildest country which I had ever
'seen. When we climbed up one side, we were
'obliged to climb down the other side on all fours.
'At various places we had to let the horses down by
'ropes, and in crossing streams we first had to
'throw a rope across. Once the current carried away
'my horses and they would have been lost had it not
'been for my Mexican servant.

'One night we camped at the foot of Mount
'Hood. We had nothing to eat but dried fish, and
'there was no grass and no water for the animals.
'However, when we started the next morning, the
'mules and horses suddenly scented water, and then
'nothing could hold them. When we arrived in the
'Willamette Mission on the ninth of September,
'six days after our departure from the mission at
'The Dalles, people would not have believed us had
'I not carried with me a letter from Mr. Perkins.
'So difficult and dangerous was this journey that
'Mr. Lee, in spite of his knowledge of the country
'and his experienced guides, arrived eight days
'later, just when the settlers were about to send out
'a relief party.

'In the Willamette Valley we rested. The mis-
'sionaries tried in vain to persuade me to settle
'there. We went from there to Fort Vancouver, this
'time going down the river in canoes. We arrived at
'the fort in the early part of October 1838, just six
'months after we had bidden farewell to our friends
'in St. Louis. I had letters from Stewart to James
'Douglas, who was then the chief factor at Fort
'Vancouver. Hence I was made welcome and was
'invited by the Governor to spend the winter among
'the hospitable Britishers. If they just hadn't
'smoked so much tobacco! I could hardly get my
'breath in their smoking room.

'I had thought of going from Fort Vancouver to
'California overland. There were many Canadians
'and other settlers, most of them former employees
'of the Hudson's Bay Company, who wanted to go
'south with me the following spring in order to buy
'cattle for their farms on the Columbia River. But
'this would have meant spending the winter at Fort
'Vancouver, and since there was a vessel about to
'sail for the Sandwich Islands, I decided to follow
'Governor Douglas's advice to take passage on her.

[16]

'As there were frequently vessels crossing from the
'Islands to California, I could hope to reach my
'destination at an earlier date. The vessel was the
'bark *Columbia* of the Hudson's Bay Company,
'whose cargo consisted of lumber for the Islands
'and furs for England.

'I took with me only two men, one of my German
'companions and an Indian boy. The others were
'to follow by the land route as soon as I had settled
'in California. The young Indian I had bought
'from Bill Brown at the Rendezvous, who in turn
'had bought him from Kit Carson. I paid for him
'with a beaver order of one hundred dollars on the
'Hudson's Bay Company. Since these beaver orders
'were worth more than their equivalent in American
'money, the boy really cost me one hundred and
'thirty dollars. This was rather a high price, but
'the Indian was very useful to me because he could
'speak English. When I sold my horses and mules
'to the settlers before embarking for the Sandwich
'Islands, I was likewise paid with beaver orders, as
'the orders on the Hudson's Bay Company were
'generally called.

[17]

'I disembarked at Honolulu on the ninth of De-
'cember, 1838. It was a Sunday when we landed,
'and I saw the natives attending church, some of
'them in silk dresses and barefooted. Lord Pelly
'and William French, an American merchant, came
'on board and invited me to stay with them. My
'German companion was a cabinet maker, who soon
'found work and made a little money during the
'stay.

'However, there seemed to be no opportunity for
'me to reach California. The *Bolivar,* Captain
'Gorham H. Neye, an old trading vessel running
'from the Islands and trading along the coast of
'California, had sailed just before I arrived. I re-
'mained five months on the Islands before I saw a
'chance of reaching my destination.'

Sutter spent the time during his unforeseen de-
tention making friends and building up his reputation. Within a few weeks he had shaken hands
with every influential person on the Islands. He
was regarded as a "Swiss gentleman and first class
man, honored for his talents and reputation," as
John C. Jones, the American consul at Oahu, wrote

to Colonel Vallejo. It was here too where Sutter realized that his rank of a bankrupt cloth merchant from an obscure Swiss town would hardly befit his ambitious scheme. He decided to stand out among the motley crowd which was annually swept upon the shores of fair California. Just as John DeKalb, the hero of the revolutionary army at Camden, had signed his own patent of nobility when he found that a Franconian peasant's son had no chances in the French army before 1789, so John Augustus Sutter promoted himself to a captaincy in the army of Charles X. Henceforth he was known and addressed as "Captain" until some fifteen years later when the legislature of California raised his rank to that of major general.

'It was not until May 1839, that my opportu-'nity finally came. The brig *Clementine*, Master 'John Blinn, which had been riding at anchor in 'the bay of Honolulu under the British flag, was 'put up for sale. Mr. French told me that he could 'guarantee enough freight money to pay for the 'whole ship, if I should decide to buy it and sail it 'to the Russian colony at New Archangel in Sitka.

'Therefore I bought the brig at a low price, loaded
'it with Mr. French's cargo of provisions and gen-
'eral merchandise, and set sail on the twentieth of
'April, 1839. After I had discharged my cargo at
'Sitka and before continuing my journey to Yerba
'Buena, I spent a pleasant month with the Rus-
'sians. The governor of the Russian colony was
'Admiral Kauprianov, and his wife was the former
'Princess of Menchikov. The Russians had many
'fast days, sometimes as many as three in one week.
'Here I could make good use of my knowledge of
'languages: with the chief clerk I spoke Spanish,
'with the storekeeper German, and with the Gov-
'ernor and his officers French. I had the honor of
'dancing with the wife of the Governor, but unfor-
'tunately I was obliged to participate in dances
'which was entirely foreign to me.'

III

Arrival in California

IT WAS at New Archangel that Sutter's scheme of colonizing the Sacramento Valley took definite shape. He had probably heard of the rich interior of the country during his sojourn in New Mexico. Ewing Young and Kit Carson had spent the summer of 1830 in the valley of California, hunting deer and fighting Indians, and their tales were current in Taos and Santa Fe. In the Russian colony his attention was certainly called to the report of Otto von Kotzebue, who had sailed the Sacramento River up to the mouth of the American River in November of 1824. He likewise must have heard there of Belcher's account of the exploration of the Sacramento River in the fall of 1837, which like other reports stressed the beauty and fertility of the interior valley of California. Finally, at Fort Vancouver Sutter had doubtless talked to trappers who knew the valley. A brigade of the Hudson's Bay Company had been there every year since Michel La Framboise, the "vivacious voyageur" who had a wife of high rank in every Indian tribe, had led the first party to the Sacramento in 1832. We may therefore assume that Sutter's mind was definitely made up as to the place of his future colony when he left Alaska towards the middle of June.

'As we were sailing down the northwest coast, the 'weather turned so bad that it seemed almost im-'possible to make our way through the narrows, 'later known as the Golden Gate. Had I not had a 'copy of Belcher's survey, which the Governor had 'been kind enough to order for me, we should not 'have been able to find the entrance. On the second 'day of July, 1839, we finally entered the Bay of 'San Francisco and anchored off Yerba Buena. An

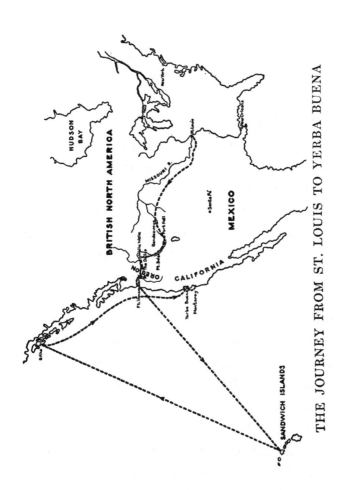

THE JOURNEY FROM ST. LOUIS TO YERBA BUENA

'officer with about fifteen Mexican soldiers came on
'board and asked me what I wanted. "This is not
'a port of entry," he said. "You cannot land here;
'you must go to Monterey."

'I told him that I knew this very well and that I
'had not entered the port intentionally, but had
'been driven into the bay by the stress of the
'weather and because I was out of provisions. For-
'tunately I had letters from Mr. French and from
'other gentlemen from the Islands and from Sitka
'for Nathan Spear, Captain Gorham Nye, and
'Captain John Wilson, the brother-in-law of Colo-
'nel Vallejo and the stepfather of the future gov-
'ernor, Romualdo Pacheco. Some of these gentle-
'men came on board and expostulated with the
'officer, saying that I ought not to be prevented
'from landing since I was in distress. By dint of
'hard talking, Captain Wilson secured permission
'for a stay of forty-eight hours, during which time
'I might land, buy provisions, and make repairs.
'Immediately I hired carpenters and sailmakers,
'and on the morning of July fourth, I was ready to
'set sail. The few Americans who had settled in

'Yerba Buena were very anxious for me to remain
'and join in the celebration of the day, but the
'authorities would not permit it.

'The next day I arrived at Monterey and
'stopped at the house of David Spence, the most
'influential foreigner at the capital. The Russians,
'who were then on friendly terms with Californians,
'as well as Governor Douglas and others, had given
'me letters of introduction to Mr. Spence and to
'Governor Alvarado. When I went with my host to
'see the Governor, the former remarked that he had
'never seen a man with so many letters of recom-
'mendation. When Alvarado heard of my plan of
'settling in the interior valley of California, he was
'very glad that some one had come to start a col-
'ony in the wilderness where the Indians were very
'wild and very bad. I intended to settle in the valley
'because a captain who had sailed up the Sacra-
'mento River for a short distance had told me much
'about the beauty and fertility of that district.
'Therefore, I asked the Governor for a grant of
'land by the Sacramento River. Alvarado advised
'me to make my selection first and to return to

'Monterey within a year in order to become a citi-
'zen. Then he would give me a grant for all unoccu-
'pied land that I might have selected.'

Governor Juan Bautista Alvarado had more
than one reason to listen to the plans of the Swiss
adventurer with amiable interest. His benevolent
attitude, however, was scarcely caused by the
twenty-odd letters of introduction which Sutter
spread out for Spence, the friendly Scotchman, to
interpret. On the contrary, recommendations from
United States consuls, Russian governors, and fac-
tors of the Hudson's Bay Company might have
aroused a certain suspicion in the Californian. But
Sutter's openhearted enthusiasm soon convinced
Alvarado that this man had not come to promote
the interest of any foreign power.

The future of California was anything but rosy
at that time. Since the eleventh of April, 1822,
when the *Junta* and the military had renounced
the Spanish sovereignty and sworn allegiance to
the revolutionary Mexican government, the semi-
independent district had shared the fate of all the
young republics established on the ruins of the

Spanish Empire in America. The constant friction
with the Mexican motherland, the bitter rivalry
among the various factions, the growing influence
of the foreign element, the potential danger of
American, Russian, or English interference, the
obvious failure to solve the Indian problem, all
this precluded a regular and stable development.
The live stock, which had amounted to one hundred and fifty thousand head of cattle, twenty
thousand horses and mules, one hundred and
ninety thousand sheep during the last years of the
Spanish rule, had decreased by fifty to seventy-five
per cent. Only a fraction of the crop of wheat,
barley, corn, and beans, which had at times
reached the respectable figure of one hundred and
eighty thousand bushels, was harvested during
the last year; less than half of the neophyte
Indians stayed with the missions.

The inauguration of a new civilization could
not be the work of the Mexican or the Californian
government but had to be left to private initiative.
What could be accomplished by a vigorous promo-
tion of colonization and a tactful Indian policy

was shown by Colonel Mariano Vallejo's settlement of Sonoma at the site of the former Mission Solano. But men of the stamp of Vallejo, since 1836 *comandante general* of California, were few among the Spanish Californians. Moreover, any native who united much power in his hands became a potential danger to the authorities at Monterey. Alvarado's interest in Sutter's scheme and his benevolent attitude toward foreigners in general were in no small measure dictated by the fear of a strong rival for the supremacy in California.

It must have been especially welcome to Alvarado that Sutter had no intention of following the example of other foreigners by settling near the coast but that he declared his firm decision of establishing his colony in the Sacramento Valley.

The settlement of the province followed a narrow strip along the coast. The rich interior valleys were inhabited exclusively by aboriginal tribes whose unquenchable habits of stealing and kidnapping were by no means tempered by a liberal admixture of former mission Indians. While these valley Indians were no real danger to the existence

[28]

of the organized government, especially after the plague of 1833 had played terrible havoc along the Sacramento and San Joaquin rivers, their never ceasing raids upon the settlements were a constant source of vexation. Less embarrassing but just as injurious to the resources of the country was the trapping by foreigners. The valley, especially the northern sector, contained an abundance of fur animals at that time. Annually the trappers of the Hudson's Bay Company entered the Sacramento Valley from Oregon and carried off a rich booty of furs and skins. No serious attempt had ever been made to stop them. In this as in every other respect the valley had remained a child of sorrow.

The idea of establishing a mission in the Sacramento Valley had been in the mind of the government ever since Fathers Abella and Fortuni had explored the lower courses of the rivers in October 1811, and had given a favorable report as to the possibilities of settling the country. In the turbulent years which followed, the plan was postponed and finally given up entirely as a result of the hostile attitude of the new government toward colonization by the Church.

However, on July twenty-ninth, 1829, just ten years before the coming of J. A. Sutter, Abel Stearns, a shrewd New Englander, had arrived from Mexico with the intention of obtaining a large tract of land in the Sacramento or San Joaquin Valley and starting a colony in conjunction with George W. Ayres. Before his project could be consummated, Don Abel became entangled in the political complications during Victoria's governorship and was expelled from the North. Five years later, on the twenty-sixth of June, 1834, the dauntless projector and promoter, Hall J. Kelley, gained Governor Figueroa's approval of a plan to explore and settle the interior valley. The fact that Sutter carried out what he had planned formed one of Kelley's many grievances in later years.

Now the right man had finally arrived to put the long cherished project into execution. If he should fail, it would be his loss; if he succeeded, his colony would become a source of revenue for the government, the inroads of the Hudson's Bay

Company would cease, the Indians would be held
in check, and Sutter's settlement might become an
effective buffer against any over-ambitious
schemes on the part of the Russians or of the
potentate of Sonoma. The change of faith, to
which most newcomers had to be induced by the
charming eyes of a native daughter, was superflu-
ous in the case of Sutter. He was a son of the Holy
Catholic Church; at least so he told the Governor.

'On the seventh of July I returned with my ves-
'sel to Yerba Buena. I anchored at the spot which
'is now the corner of Clay and Montgomery
'Streets. The nearest house to my anchorage,
'within about fifty yards of my vessel, was the
'store of Spear and Hinkley. There was a large
'one-story adobe building at the upper side of the
'plaza, where Dupont Street now runs. This was
'the property of the Englishman, William Rich-
'ardson, the captain of the port, who had built the
'first tent at the Yerba Buena cove in 1835. The
'following year Jacob Leese had come and built a
'fine frame building on Montgomery Street. This
'place was later sold to the Hudson's Bay Com-

'pany for a store. There were a few other small
'houses: one, a little frame house, belonging to
'John Fuller, situated a little above Mr. Spear's,
'near Sacramento Street, and also a little adobe be-
'longing to Victor Prudon, a Frenchman, who did
'some trading and sold liquor by the drink. He was
'a good Spanish scholar, and often he drew up
'papers for the government and for the settlers.
'His house was at Montgomery Street near Tele-
'graph Hill. There was no wharf as yet and where
'the fort building now stands at the Golden Gate,
'there was nothing. The *Presidio* was manned by a
'small garrison of Mexican soldiers, and was armed
'with a few guns, which did not look as if they
'could do much damage.

'The Mission Dolores under Padre Jose Gutier-
'rez was likewise in a state of stagnation. A few
'people were living there on surrounding farms
'and attended church at the Mission. They were
'mostly native Californians and a few Indians.
'The stock of cattle and horses was very small.
'The government had disposed of practically all
'the property of the Mission and had pocketed the

'money. Everything had been sold very cheaply:
'the Hudson's Bay Company had once procured a
'lot of sheep at fifty cents a head. Young cattle
'were worth about three dollars each; stallions, ten
'dollars; and mares, three to four dollars. Stal-
'lions were worth more because they were broken,
'while the mares were mostly wild and used ex-
'clusively for breeding.

'I had only little freight when I landed at Yerba
'Buena. Since my vessel was altogether too large
'for use on the Sacramento River, I settled my ac-
'count with the Russians and with Mr. French,
'supplied the ship with the necessary provisions,
'and sent her back in charge of Captain Blinn,
'who had sailed with me from the Islands, with a
'request to Mr. French to sell her for me.

'I then chartered from Spear and Hinkley the
'schooner *Isabella*, Master "Kanaka" Jack Rains-
'ford, of about twenty tons, and a yacht, which
'had once been a pleasure boat belonging to the
'king of the Sandwich Islands and which had been
'brought, I believe, by Captain Hinkley on board
'of another vessel. This boat, called the *Nicholas*,

[33]

'was in command of William H. Davis, who repre-
'sented the firm of Spear and Hinkley. Finally,
'I bought a small pinnace from Captain Wilson.

'The crew of my vessels consisted of the two
'German carpenters I had brought with me from
'the Islands, and a number of sailors and me-
'chanics I had picked up at Yerba Buena. I also
'had eight Kanakas, all experienced seamen, whom
'King Kamehameha had given me when I left the
'Sandwich Islands. I had undertaken to pay them
'ten dollars a month and to send them back to the
'Islands after three years at my own expense if
'they wished to leave me. These men were very
'glad to go with me, and at the expiration of their
'time, they showed no inclination to return to their
'people. Two of them were married and brought
'their wives with them. These women made them-
'selves very useful by teaching the Indian girls to
'wash, sew, and do other practical things. As it will
'appear further on, I could not have settled the
'country without the aid of these Kanakas. They
'were always faithful and loyal to me.

'After I had sent the *Clementine* back to the

'Sandwich Islands and before I acquired my little
'fleet, I paid visits to Colonel Vallejo at Sonoma
'and to Fort Ross. Toward the end of July I went
'to Sonoma in a row boat with a crew belonging to
'Captain Wilson. The latter, as well as Captain
'Richardson, accompanied me, waited for me while
'I went to Fort Ross, and took me back to Yerba
'Buena.

'Colonel Vallejo ranked then as *comandante*
'*general*, commanding a garrison of about fifty
'men. The Mission Solano, in charge of Padre Jose
'Quijas, consisted of a church building, several
'out-houses, and a few Indian huts. Vallejo's new
'residence was not yet finished. The soldiers had
'their barracks in the mission buildings. I went to
'Sonoma to pay my respects to the colonel, as well
'as to get acquainted with the country. Vallejo
'told me that it would not be necessary for me to
'go as far as the Sacramento Valley, because there
'was plenty of unoccupied land near the Bay. He
'mentioned Suisun, Monte Diablo, the Napa Val-
'ley, and many other places. But I declined and
'said that I preferred to settle by a navigable

'river. This, however, was only an excuse; my real
'object was to get away from the influence of the
'Spaniards.

'Captain Wilson owned a *rancho* in Sonoma
'Valley with a large stock of cattle, which he
'offered me at a very low price. When I again de-
'clined, he exclaimed angrily: "Well, my God, I
' "should like to know what you really want!"
'They were surprised that I should decline their
'favorable offers and go alone into the wilderness.
'I had noticed very well that one's hat had to be
'taken off before the military guard, the flag-staff,
'and the church. I preferred a country where I
'could keep my hat on; in other words, I wanted to
'be my own master. I also had information that the
'people of this valley had a way of marking other
'people's cattle, a practice which I did not like
'very much.

'Accompanied by a *vaquero*, I left the next day
'for Fort Ross. At the Mackintosh farm, near
'Bodega, I got fresh horses and went with these
'to the first Russian station, about midway be-
'tween Bodega and Fort Ross. This station was a

'kind of a farm with two wooden houses. In one
'of these houses, a room was set apart for travelers.
'Here one could rest for the night without charge,
'receive a good meal, and continue the journey the
'next morning on fresh horses. The *vaquero* from
'Sonoma remained here and a Russian accompa-
'nied me to Fort Ross. At the Fort I was well
'received by the governor, Baron Alexander
'Rotchev, for whom I had letters from the gover-
'nor of Sitka. Lady Rotchev was born a princess
'of Gagarin. Since there had been difficulties in the
'way of a conventional marriage, the Baron had
'eloped with her. The place consisted of about fifty
'timber houses, mostly one-story buildings occu-
'pied by mechanics and laborers in the employ of
'the colonial service. There were a tannery, black-
'smith, tailor, shoe-maker shops, and other indus-
'tries. The Russian governor had granted the
'Californians the privilege of buying articles here.
'The settlement had been established mostly for
'seal and sea-otter hunting, but now agricultural
'interests were predominant. There were a great
'many farms in the vicinity, all belonging to the

'Russians. They raised wheat, barley, and vegeta-
'bles, as well as cattle and horses. The Russians
'in Alaska were supplied with provisions from this
'settlement. The governor of Sitka had two cows,
'but the hay had to be brought up from Fort Ross.
'Besides the Russians the colony employed a large
'number of California Indians. Fort Ross was sub-
'ordinate to the governor of Sitka. Besides the
'dwellings there was a large wooden Greek church
'at Fort Ross. The whole settlement was sur-
'rounded by a wooden wall of split and hewed
'timber, about eighteen feet high and one or two
'feet thick.

'The Fort was beautifully situated on a rock
'overlooking the ocean, and in stormy weather the
'waves dashed up against the walls and the build-
'ings. In the beautiful garden behind the Fort was
'a nice garden-house about twenty feet square with
'glass windows and doors. When I purchased the
'place some time later, Madame Rotchev begged
'me not to destroy the garden house which she had
'built and in which she had spent so many happy
'hours. I endeavored to comply with her request

'and removed it in sections to Sacramento. How-
'ever, when my men attempted to set it up there in
'its original form, they could not put it together
'because they did not understand the workmanship
'of the Russian carpenters and I had to use it for
'other purposes.

'I told the Governor of my intention to settle in
'the Sacramento Valley, and he asked me to call
'on him if he could be of any service to me. After
'taking dinner with him, I returned to the Mack-
'intosh farm where I spent the night. The next
'day I was back in Sonoma and returned from
'there to Yerba Buena.'

IV

The Beginnings of New Helvetia

'AFTER my return I prepared everything for my
'trip to the Sacramento. I stocked the boats with
'provisions, agricultural implements, blacksmith
'and carpenter tools, muskets and rifles, arms and
'ammunition, and three cannon.

'On the first of August, 1839, I was ready to
'set sail. Before my departure I accepted an invi-
'tation to dine on board a large American trading
'vessel of about four hundred tons. The name of
'the ship I have forgotten; her captain was James
'P. Arther. The captains of all the vessels in port,
'as well as the principal settlers of Yerba Buena,

'were present. All had come to bid me good-by, for
'none expected to see me again.

'From this ship, I stepped down the rope ladder
'into my small pinnace, which was rowed by Ka-
'nakas, and ordered the two other vessels to follow
'me. When I reached Suisun, I stopped at Mar-
'tinez' *rancho*, situated at the junction of the Bay
'and the Straits of Carquinez. I made arrange-
'ments with Martinez for a supply of horses and
'cattle. After I had entered Suisun Bay, it took
'me several days to find the mouth of the Sacra-
'mento River. I explored all the sloughs around
'there, went up the San Joaquin River as far as
'the site of the present city of Stockton, but was
'always obliged to return to the Suisun Bay. One
'night after sundown, after having searched again
'all day in vain, I said, disgruntled, to my people:
' "Now let us go in here and camp for the night."
'But when we entered the slough which I had se-
'lected, I suddenly saw a wide opening and knew
'at once that this was the river.

'The Sacramento received its name from the
'pious Franciscan fathers who went up the rivers

'short distances in search for wild Indians whom
'they wanted to convert. In May 1817, Padre
'Narciso Duran of the Mission San Jose under-
'took such an expedition and succeeded in baptiz-
'ing a number of women and infants who had not
'been able to escape at the approach of the barge.
'He sailed as far as the *rancheria* of the Chu-
'cumnes who were soon to become my subjects.

'The next morning I entered the river, again
'preceding the two larger vessels in my small boat.
'I entered and explored all the sloughs, leaving
'marks and fastening notes to the branches of the
'trees in order to tell my men in which direction
'to sail and which places to avoid. All along the
'shore I noticed signs of Indians. On the overhang-
'ing branches of trees the natives had tied bunches
'of white feathers, symbols of prayers to gods and
'devils for fish and food.

'Although I knew that I was being closely
'watched from the shore all along my journey, I
'did not encounter a single Indian until I reached
'a point on the river about twelve miles below the
'site of the present city of Sacramento. We arrived

'at this point on the second day after we had left
'Suisun Bay, and here I suddenly saw in an open
'space about two hundred warriors. They were
'painted yellow, black, and red and seemed to be
'very keen for a fight. My men wanted to fire at
'them at once, but I ordered them to keep quiet
'and to make no attack until I gave them the
'order. The two larger vessels were still some dis-
'tance behind me. We approached the shore in the
'rowboat and I jumped on land unarmed and
'alone. I had instructed my men to stand ready
'with their arms concealed, but not to fire until
'they saw me attacked. Thinking that there might
'be among the Indians some who had escaped from
'the missions and who understood Spanish, I
'shouted in a loud voice: "*Adios, amigos!*" I was
'not disappointed. Immediately two of them came
'forward and answered in Spanish. I told them
'that I had not come to them to make war or to
'carry them off to the missions, but that I had
'come to live among them as a friend. One of these
'mission Indians I sent in a canoe with a letter to
'my vessels downstream, and the other I took with

'me in my boat as a guide. After the two Indians
'had told their brothers that they were to come
'to me after my landing and receive presents, they
'all appeared to be satisfied and went away to their
'village. I continued on my way, passed the mouth
'of the American River, and went as far as the
'mouth of the Feather River. There was a large
'Indian *rancheria,* whose inhabitants, men, women,
'and children, took to their heels when they saw us
'coming.

'Since the Feather River is wider at its mouth
'than the Sacramento, I mistook it for the latter
'and traveled upstream ten or fifteen miles before
'I became convinced that I was not on the Sacra-
'mento. Hence, I returned to the mouth of the
'Feather River where I found my two vessels at
'anchor. My men were greatly fatigued from row-
'ing and I was extremely tired myself. Since night
'had fallen in the meantime, I went on board the
'schooner, which had a little cabin. As I was enter-
'ing it, the men demanded to know how long I was
'going to take them about the wilderness in this

'manner. I told them that they would receive an
'answer in the morning.

'During the night I thought the matter over.
'I had wished to explore the country further up,
'but I knew that I could do nothing with mutinous
'men. So I told them the next morning that I had
'decided to return. We floated down to the mouth
'of the American River and sailed up that stream
'as far as the boats could go. Then I gave orders to
'land everything. I pitched tents and mounted my
'cannons.

'When I noticed increased dissatisfaction among
'the white men, I determined to put an end to it.
'As soon as everything was on shore, I called all
'hands together and informed them that the next
'morning I should send the schooner to Yerba
'Buena. I told them that they were free to go down
'on her, for I wanted to have none but contented
'men around me, even at the risk of being left
'alone with my Kanakas. I said that every one's
'pay was ready. Six of them decided to return,
'and during the night I drew orders on Nathan

'Spear for their pay. There was no money in cir-
'culation then, and Mr. Spear would pay them in
'goods. Hides were the principal currency, valued
'at a dollar fifty in cash and two dollars in trade.
'Articles on trading vessels were so high that it
'was said a man could carry away his purchase
'in a pocket handkerchief if he would go on board
'with a hundred dollars in money or in hides. I
'always sent Mr. Spear furs and drew orders on
'him. There were plenty of beaver and otter skins,
'the former being worth four dollars and the latter
'three dollars a pound, as well as elk and deer
'skins. When I chartered my vessels, however, I
'paid for them in American and Mexican money.

'My object in sending the schooner down was to
'obtain a supply of provisions. It is hardly
'necessary to state that my men did not return
'because they were afraid of the Indians, but be-
'cause they were not willing to stand the discom-
'forts of the wilderness. After I was fairly well
'settled, there was never any lack of laborers.

'I was now left with my eight Kanakas, three
'white men, and one Indian. Since we were in need

'of some meat, I sent one of the white men and the
'Indian on a hunt, and they soon returned with an
'elk. After that there was never any lack of meat.
'Flour, beans, and other provisions, however, I had
'to get from Mr. Spear at Yerba Buena. Dried
'beef was in those days a regular article of com-
'merce, and I used to get it at two or three cents a
'pound.

'The Indians came forward now and received
'the presents which I had promised them. I pre-
'sented them with beads, blankets, and shirts, and
'they seemed to be well satisfied. They brought
'some horses with sore backs, which they had stolen
'from settlers. I bought them at a very low price,
'pastured them until they were well, and then re-
'turned them to the owners for the price which I
'had paid. To show the Indians the effect of ball
'and powder, I had my guns fired at a target.
'They naturally showed no inclination to have the
'guns trained on them.'

When the *Isabella* and the *Nicholas* weighed
anchor the next morning, Sutter's cannon fired a
salute of nine guns. While the deer and elk, fright-

ened by the unusual detonation, fled terror-
stricken, and the timber wolves and coyotes in the
woods set up a howl, the two ships glided into the
stream and the crews replied to the salute by three
rousing cheers.

Thus began the history of New Helvetia. The
date on the calendar was Monday, August the
thirteenth, 1839.

'From the landing I went back about a quarter
'of a mile to the spot where the Fort subsequently
'stood, now within the limits of the city of Sacra-
'mento, not far from the capitol. I selected the
'highest ground I could find. The Kanakas first
'erected two grass houses after the manner of the
'houses on the Sandwich Islands; the frames were
'made by white men and covered with grass by the
'Kanakas. These houses were very comfortable.
'Next I built a one-story building of adobe. This
'house was about forty feet long and contained a
'blacksmith shop, a kitchen, and a room for myself.
'It was covered with tule and was completed just
'before the autumn rains set in. In the spring I
'had my men make a large quantity of adobe

SUTTER IN HIS FORTIES

FORT ROSS

Water-color drawing by G. J. Denny

MISSION BUENA VENTURA

Drawing by E. Vischer

'bricks for the walls of the Fort and for the other 'buildings. I also had a quantity of lumber cut and 'sawed up into boards. The white men taught the 'Indians the use of the whip-saw and of other im-'plements. In addition to the white men, the Ka-'nakas, and the Indians, a few Californians were 'employed by me as *vaqueros;* two of them were 'engaged in building carts of the type used in 'California at that time.

'During the winter we also cut a road through 'the woods and fixed up a landing place, the new '*embarcadero,* where the old Zinns' House now 'stands. Soon it was time to make a garden and to 'sow some wheat after the soil had been broken 'with the poor California plows.'

The question of securing the initial live stock and the seed for the first year's crop was the most pressing problem for the newcomer. Sutter's cash was long exhausted, everything had to be bought on credit, and years might pass before any substantial profits could be reaped.

Captain Wilson had promised Sutter thirty-four young cows and a bull, while a small quantity of grain was secured from Antonio Soto at San Jose. However, the main source of supply for the first few months was Ignacio Martinez at Pinole, the nearest neighbor. During September and October Sutter received from Pinole ten milk cows with their calves, four yoke of oxen, one breeding bull, twenty-five young unbroken oxen for killing, as well as a few *fanegas* of wheat, corn, and beans. But when Sutter was slow in paying, the old Mexican soldier discontinued his deliveries, and he complained to Vallejo when Nathan Spear, Sutter's banker at Yerba Buena, did not honor his client's warrant. Not until December 1840, after many harsh words had passed, could Martinez certify that the debt had been paid in full. It was the first of the many tragi-comic episodes in the business dealings of the Lord of New Helvetia.

Sutter's other neighbor—if such he might be called—lived some seventy-five miles distant. He was John Marsh, Doctor of Medicine and, since 1837, owner of the *rancho Pulpunes*, at the foot of Monte Diablo. Dr. Marsh was not as amenable to extending credit to the newcomer as the

merchants of Yerba Buena or Don Ignacio, although—or perhaps just because—he had met
Sutter at Independence in 1835. However, the
Captain possessed a veritable treasure in a brand
new book on the medical sciences, and hardly had
the close-fisted and close-mouthed New Englander
heard of this book than he set his heart on it.
Whether he believed that his own medical knowledge had become rusty, or whether he was angry
because Sutter cured all kinds of diseases with its
help, sending him only the very serious or hopeless
cases, he tried every means to wheedle the book
out of him. But Sutter was loath to part with it.
The doctor volunteered to deliver horses and cattle
against future payment. Sutter gratefully accepted but unfortunately the medical book had
mysteriously disappeared. The Harvard graduate
loaned the Captain a book on practical agriculture; Sutter studied it carefully and returned it
with thanks, but at this particular time there was
so much sickness around New Helvetia that Sutter
simply could not do without his medical tome.
Sutter finally promised in November 1841, to send

it with Robert Livermore, but at the last minute found that Livermore had so much luggage of his own it would have been an imposition to put the heavy book on top of it.

Dr. Marsh had to practice his profession without the aid of the invaluable book, and the relations between the two pioneers never became very cordial. Their business transactions were always hampered by a sincere distrust of each other, and at times they did not refrain from telling their friends unpleasant stories of old Missouri days.

'For the cattle and horses which I had pur-'chased from Señor Martinez, I had to wait a long 'time. The stock finally arrived on the twenty-'second of October, 1839, accompanied by not less 'than eight men because they were afraid of the 'Indians and had doubtless good reason to be so.

'In the meantime the schooner made frequent 'trips between my place and Yerba Buena. It was 'a dangerous journey and usually took us eight or 'ten days. It is surprising that we did not get 'swamped many a time in our open boat, especially 'as the crew consisted of inexperienced Indians

'with a Kanaka at the helm. Once it took me six-
'teen days to get down to Yerba Buena and back,
'and when I went down to the bay on the twenty-
'second of December, 1839, the weather was so bad
'and the current of the river so strong that the
'return trip took up seventeen days, and nearly
'all the provisions were spoiled.

'When my settlement became known, a good
'many men came up and asked for employment.
'Runaway sailors, mountaineers, and other people
'wanted to hunt for me or to work at their trade.
'Many of them were of no value to me. Very glad
'was I, on the other hand, when on August seven-
'teenth, 1840, some of the men with whom I had
'crossed the Rocky Mountains two years before
'arrived at my settlement. The American trader
'*Lausanne* had picked them up in Oregon, together
'with William Wiggins and Peter Lassen, and had
'disembarked them at Bodega. When they told
'the Russian governor that they wanted to join
'me, they were received very kindly and hospitably
'and furnished with fine horses and new saddles at
'a very low rate. The Russians also told them

[53]

'which route to take in order not to fall into the
'hands of the Spaniards, who would probably have
'imprisoned them at Sonoma. I was, of course, very
'glad to employ these men and thereby strengthen
'my position. In the fall of 1840, I had about
'twenty white men working for me in addition to a
'large number of natives.

'The Indians were sometimes troublesome, but
'on the whole I got along very nicely with them.
'One night, however, an attempt was made to as-
'sassinate me. I was sitting talking to my clerk,
'Octavio Custot, a former French sailor and my
'right hand man during the first few years, when
'about midnight, I heard some one cry: "Oh,
'Señor!" The clerk ran out to ascertain the cause
'and found an Indian in the teeth of a bulldog
'which I had brought with me from the Sandwich
'Islands. The Indian had hardly been brought into
'the house, when a similar cry was heard and a
'second fellow was caught in the same manner.
'It appeared that a whole band of Indians had
'come to kill all of us and to seize my settlement.
'The watchfulness of the dog had prevented the

'carrying out of their intentions. I sewed up the
'wounds of the savages and told them I would
'forgive them this time but that any further at-
'tempts in the same direction would be met with
'swift punishment. Nevertheless, the same winter
'we caught a number of Indians, who had their
'weapons concealed in the very blankets which I
'had given them. When I asked them why they
'wanted to kill me, who had treated them well, they
'answered that they simply wanted to plunder.

'During the next summer the Indians showed
'fight. They withdrew en masse to a place at the
'Cosumnes River about twenty miles away from
'their village near the settlement. I took this for a
'sign of hostility and attacked them during the
'night with six of my men. After we had killed
'six of their number, they ceased their resistance
'and asked for mercy. None of my men had been
'killed or wounded. I told them that everything
'would be forgotten if they would come back to
'the village and attend to their work as before.
'After this the Chucumnes Indians, who lived in
'the territory of my settlement, caused me no fur-

'ther trouble but became my faithful servants. I
'taught them how to work and paid them for their
'services. Later I adopted a tin currency impressed
'with a stamp made by my blacksmith, Samuel
'Neal, who had left Frémont and entered my serv-
'ices. This currency showed a star and had holes,
'each of which represented one day's work. With
'this money they could buy at my store blankets
'or any other thing that they required. White men
'tried to cheat the Indians out of this money in
'various ways, but I refused to accept it from any
'one but the natives.

'Next I bought orphan boys from other tribes,
'instructed them in the Spanish language, and
'taught them how to work. The best looking In-
'dians I organized as a military company, one
'hundred men infantry and fifty horsemen. The
'former were officered by two white men and an
'Indian chief. Another officer who served as an en-
'sign was born in a mission and could read and
'write. His name was Homobono. The Spaniards
'were very much surprised when they saw my In-

'dian soldiers, especially because one of them could
'read and write, which was more than could be said
'of many Californians. Later on they were also
'surprised when they saw my Fort with cannon
'mounted on bastions.

'The distant tribes, however, continued to look
'upon my establishment as an object for pillaging,
'and I had to undertake several campaigns against
'these Indians, in most cases as a punishment for
'stealing cattle. But finally I had subjugated all
'the Indians in the Sacramento Valley, and was
'often in a position to render valuable assistance
'to the other settlers. When Peter Lassen, who had
'a farm in the upper part of the valley, was at
'one time attacked by the Indians, he sent to me for
'help. I went with about thirty-five men and three
'hundred Indians. We attacked them at night
'after my Indian trappers had made rafts and had
'gone to the other side of the river. Some of the
'Indians were killed and the rest were captured.

'Once a band of Cosumnes Indians came to me
'with a pass from the Mission San Jose and asked

'my permission to trade with the Indians in the 'mountains on the American River. Sensing no 'peril, I granted their request. But instead of trad-'ing with the Indians in the mountains, they killed 'a number of them and seized their women and 'children. The women they wanted to keep for 'themselves, and the children they intended to sell 'to the Spaniards. It was a common practice in 'those days to seize women and children in order 'to sell them. This was done by the Californians as 'well as by the Indians.

'I learned of this outrage from an old man who 'had escaped, and immediately set out with about 'twenty of my men and a host of Indians. I en-'countered them about thirty miles below New Hel-'vetia at the lake which is connected with the 'Sacramento River. In the name of the Govern-'ment I ordered them to surrender. Most of them 'did, and those who tried to escape were fired upon 'and finally captured. Fourteen confessed to the 'crime of murder, and I ordered them shot on the 'spot. When I informed the Government of these 'happenings, I received its thanks for my actions.

'The Indians were naturally delighted when their
'wives and children were returned to them.

'When I came into the valley, polygamy was
'still prevalent among the Indians. Since the chiefs
'had so many wives, the young men complained
'that they could not find any. I determined to put
'a stop to it. I placed the men in one row and the
'girls in a row opposite them. Then I told the
'women to come forward, one after another, and
'select a husband. To the chiefs I allowed no more
'than one or, at most, two wives.

'The last Indian campaign I had to undertake
'just before the outbreak of the Mexican War. At
'that time the natives were encouraged by the
'Mexicans to attack the settlers, as one Indian
confessed to me. The Mokelumnes, christianized
'Indians formerly belonging to the missions, at-
'tacked me one night in large numbers. By quick
'action I frightened them away. In pursuing them
'we had to cross the Mokelumne in a raft which
'was upset, and everything on it was lost. After
'we had finally overtaken them, a hard fight fol-
'lowed. Many of my men were wounded, though

'none killed. When the enemy took to the ravines 'and rocks and my ammunition became short, we 'were obliged to retire, keeping up a rifle fire as 'we withdrew from the scene.'

V

The Building of the Fort and the Purchase of the Russian Colonies

WITH the exception of these Indian troubles, nothing occurred to disturb the development of the colony during the first few years. The so-called Graham affair of April 1840, during which some fifty foreigners were deported for a real or suspected conspiracy, cast no wave on the isolated New Helvetia. Sutter continued in the good graces of the Government, although Vallejo, as well as Captain José Castro, prefect of the Monterey district, felt rather uneasy about the ambitious scheme of the Swiss.

In August of the same year Sutter went to Monterey to complete his naturalization. On the twenty-ninth of August, he took his oath as a Mexican citizen, and on September first, his appointment as judge and representative of the Government on the frontiers at the *Rio Sacramento* was signed by Jimeno Casarin, the secretary of state.

The following year was destined to become one of the most important in the history of New Helvetia. The colony had outgrown its experimental stage and was looked upon as the cradle of a new political order by American, English, and French visitors. The founder of New Helvetia had become in many respects the most important figure in the territory.

In June of this year Sutter, who in his narrative mistakenly placed his naturalization on the same date, went to Monterey to receive the promised land grant from Governor Alvarado. "He has sufficiently demonstrated his industry, good conduct, and other qualifications required in such cases; and he has already in advance manifested,

[62]

by his great efforts and constant firmness, a truly
patriotic zeal for our institutions, civilizing a
large number of savage Indians, natives of those
frontiers"—so attested the instrument of the title
deed, executed on the eighteenth of June. The
grant consisted of eleven square leagues, the
largest amount permissible by law. Thus by a
stroke of the pen Sutter became the lawful owner
of a wide stretch of fertile ground between 39° 41'
45" and 38° 41' 32" latitude, bordered on the west
by the Sacramento, on the east by a line running
from one to three miles east of the bank of the
Feather River.

'In 1841 I went down to Monterey to obtain
'from Governor Alvarado the grant which he had
'promised me. With two *vaqueros* and two armed
'men as an escort, and with thirty horses I crossed
'the valley to Livermore Pass, named after Robert
'Livermore, who had settled there a few years be-
'fore. At the Mission San Jose I obtained fresh
'horses and continued my journey to Monterey,
'stopping at the missions on my way. Governor Al-
'varado gave me a grant of eleven leagues, and I

'became a Mexican citizen. I received at the same
'time a commission as representative of the Gov-
'ernment and was entrusted also with judicial
'powers, *representante del govierno y encargado
'de las justicia.* Alvarado was afraid to give me a
'military title for fear of Vallejo; such a title I re-
'ceived later from Micheltorena. Nevertheless,
'from that time on I had power of life and death
'both over Indians and white people in my district.

'In Monterey I hired some new recruits, about
'half a dozen men, mostly mechanics. Among them
'was a negro, a good cooper and the first darky
'who ever came to the valley. When I was ready to
'return, I gathered my people in front of Mr.
'Spence's house. When several ship captains, who
'happened to be present, saw my motley crew, they
'exclaimed: "My God! How can you manage such
'vagabonds!" I told them that I got along well
'with them, because I gave them nothing to drink
'but water. During the first few years my men
'could actually get no intoxicating liquor at the
'settlement, although every Christmas and every
'Fourth of July they wanted a barrel of whiskey

'or something else to drink. When I once complied
'with their wish, they behaved so badly that I told
'them that it would be the first and the last time.
'However, the next holiday they united and threat-
'ened to leave me in a body if I did not provide
'them with something to drink. One of the men, a
'sailor, advised me not to press the point too far
'but to give them their drink and to go hunting
'for a few days; when I should return, everything
'would be all right again. I was wise to follow his
'advice. Later I built a brandy distillery and sup-
'plied trappers and settlers with liquor. The still
'was built just before Frémont arrived in distress.
'Frémont, Kit Carson, Preuss, and the rest of them
'were glad to get a civilized drink fresh from the
'distillery.

'After my return from Monterey I started to
'build a fort as a protection against the Indians
'as well as against the Californians, who had be-
'come jealous of my establishment. I built a large
'house near the first adobe building, which had
'burned down during the winter. This building I
'surrounded with walls eighteen feet high, enclosing

'altogether seventy-five thousand square feet. The
'walls were made of adobe bricks and were about
'two and a half feet thick. At two corners I built
'bastions with walls five feet thick; under these
'bastions were the prisons. Within the enclosure I
'erected other buildings; barracks for the soldiers,
'workshops and dwellings, a bakery, a mill, and a
'blanket factory. The tannery was built on the
'spot where I had first landed, and for years after-
'ward this place was known as The Tannery.
'There were several outhouses for *vaqueros* and
'other employees, which were later occupied by
'immigrants. It took four years altogether to com-
'plete the fort. It was armed by twelve cannon
'which were kept in good order by an old sailor
'who had served under Lord Cochrane in the wars
'of South America.

'I kept military discipline at the settlement, but
'there was at first neither church nor school. No
'work was done on Sunday, of course, but no at-
'tention was given to religious ceremonies by any-
'body. There was no clergy, and at burials and
'marriages I officiated myself. I was everything—

'patriarch, priest, father, and judge. Church bells
'I brought later on from the Greek church at Fort
'Ross, and had them rung at funerals.

'My personal guard consisted of about twelve
'or fifteen men, mounted Indians under the com-
'mand of a very intelligent sergeant. The guard
'room was near my bedroom so that I could be
'notified at once if anything happened. I had a
'half-hour glass installed, and during the night the
'guards struck the bell every time the sand ran out,
'and cried, "All is well!" Summer and winter at
'daybreak, the bell was rung for all hands to get
'up and go to work. Some Americans complained
'of such early rising, but I convinced them that it
'was better to get an early start and to rest dur-
'ing the hot hours at noon. We lived very simply,
'roast beef and vegetables being our principal
'dishes. Sometimes we would not get any coffee,
'and at times there was not a single lump of sugar
'in the house. We found that peas were a good sub-
'stitute for coffee, but still better we liked acorns
'from which we made a drink which was hard to
'distinguish from coffee. Tea was not very popular

'at the Fort. The Indians received daily rations of
'beef and bread, and in addition, mush was cooked
'for them in a large kettle. When I traveled, I
'lived on jerked meat and drank cold water.

'I had at first only one flour mill at the fort,
'and since an enormous amount of wheat had to be
'ground, the mill as well as the bakery were kept
'going day and night. The mill was turned by four
'mules, which were changed every four hours. A
'report of the conditions at the Fort and my mode
'of living was given to President Polk by Major
'Hensley, who escorted Commodore Stockton
'across the Rocky Mountains.

'The Indian boys were obliged to appear every
'Sunday morning for drill, well washed and neatly
'clad. Their uniform consisted of blue drill panta-
'loons, white cotton shirts, and red handkerchiefs
'tied around their heads. They were very proud of
'this uniform. After drill they could visit their
'friends at the Indian villages, or spend the day
'as they pleased. The grown-up soldiers had regu-
'lar uniforms of blue or green cloth with red trim-

'mings. These uniforms I received from the Rus-
'sians.

'In my intercourse with American settlers,
'mountaineers, and trappers, I was frank and un-
'conventional. I greeted them with a hearty hand-
'shake, although I always expected to be treated
'with respect. But with Californians and Mexicans
'I was more particular: I required them to pay the
'same deference to me as they were accustomed to
'pay to their own officers. Whenever they came
'within the walls of the Fort, they were obliged to
'take off their hats, soldiers as well as officers.
'When the Mexicans came to look for Frémont,
'they found sentries at the gate of the Fort and a
'guard at my door. Their officers, whom I quar-
'tered within the walls, asked me politely and
'humbly to permit their servants to enter the Fort.
'I gave this permission but did not let any soldiers
'inside the walls. These officers asked me one eve-
'ning whether I had built the Fort solely as a pro-
'tection against the Indians. I told them truthfully
'that the Fort was intended also as a protection

'against the Californians. Vallejo and others were
'jealous of my settlement and resented my giving
'passports to all people who came from the north
'or the east. I was friendly with the immigrants
'and encouraged immigration wherever I could,
'while the Mexicans disliked the Americans and
'were afraid of the increased immigration.

'I gave names to many of the streams in Cali-
'fornia. The name American River I derived from
'*El Paso de los Americanos*, a pass over which the
'Canadian trappers, called *Americanos* by the
'Spanish speaking Indians, used to come into the
'valley. The term Feather River, *Rio de las
'Plumas*, I selected because the Indians at the
'river decorated themselves profusely with feathers
'and because there were piles of feathers lying
'about everywhere from which the Indians made
'blankets. The geese in this district flew in such
'dense flocks that one rifle shot would frequently
'bring down two or three. I have never seen such a
'profitable hunting ground for geese, ducks, etc.
'The Indians were fat and sleek, for they lived
'much better than their brothers in the Rocky

'Mountains. The name Yuba River I derived from
'the Yuba Indians who lived there, just as many
'other streams like the Cosumnes, Mokelumne, etc.,
'had been named after Indian tribes. In the north,
'it was Bidwell who provided the streams with
'names.

'On the twenty-third of August, 1841, I had the
'opportunity to welcome the first official visitors
'from the United States. J. Ringgold, Lieutenant
'U. S. N. and commander of the *Porpoise*, ar-
'rived at the *embarcadero* with a party of Wilkes'
'great exploring expedition. The detachment con-
'sisted of seven officers and fifty men, who arrived
'in six whale boats and one launch. I received in-
'formation of their coming long before they had
'reached the landing place. Whenever strangers
'came into the valley, my Indians gave me notice
'of their approach, telling me whether they were
'white men, as they called the Americans, or Cali-
'fornians, and always giving me a good description
'of their appearance. When my scouts informed
'me of the arrival of Ringgold's flotilla, I immedi-
'ately dispatched a clerk to establish the identity

'of the visitors. The clerk was very glad when he 'saw the American flag. I at once sent down saddle 'horses for the officers and fired a salute when they 'arrived at the Fort. They were very much sur-'prised to find a flourishing settlement in this wil-'derness, and it made a very good impression upon 'the Indians to see so many white men visiting me. 'Charles Pickering, the naturalist, remained with 'me over night; the rest of the party returned to 'their camp. Ringgold was surveying the Sacra-'mento River, and the following day he continued 'his journey upstream, going as far as the Buttes. 'Two of his men had deserted and Lieutenant 'Ringgold requested me to arrest them, but I could 'not find them. Afterwards they came out of their 'hiding places, and I employed one of them in my 'tannery.'

While Lieutenant Ringgold stopped again at Sutter's on his return from the upper Sacramento, a momentous event took place.

On the afternoon of the fourth of September, the Russian schooner *Constantine* arrived at Fort Sutter's landing. Governor Rotchev had come to offer the sale of the Russian holdings in California to the Duke of New Helvetia.

Almost twenty-nine years to the day, the Russian flag had waved over Fort Ross; on the very same day on which Napoleon's advance guard had reached the walls of the holy city of Moscow in 1812, this outpost of the far-flung Russian Empire had been dedicated. But what might have become the nucleus of a new province, a province more beautiful and productive than any of the Russian lands between the Njemen and the Klondike, had remained a step-child. For over a year negotiations to sell the colony had been going on with the Hudson's Bay Company, with Colonel Vallejo, with the Mexican government, and with Sutter himself. The Russians had obviously grown tired of the business and without bothering to fight for the title to the land—which neither the Spanish nor the Mexican government had ever recognized—were willing to sell the buildings, the chattels, the live stock, throwing the twenty-ton schooner *Constantine* into the bargain, for the ridiculously low sum of thirty thousand dollars.

'Captain Ringgold visited me again on his re-
'turn trip and while he was in his camp near my
'Fort, Governor Alexander Rotchev arrived
'aboard a Russian schooner. He had come to offer
'the Russian colonies in California for sale. The
'vicinity of Fort Ross had not proved to be a good
'wheat country, furs were getting scarce, and the
'expenses were greater than the income. This was
'the first time that I had heard that the Russians
'intended to sell their settlements, and I was sur-
'prised that they had come to me. The Russians
'were not on good terms with the Californians at
'that time, and the Governor at Sitka had in-
'structed Rotchev to offer the colonies to me first.
'An agent, Peter Kostromitinov, had been sent to
'complete arrangements.

'The Governor told me that Vallejo, Leese, and
'others were ready to purchase the colonies, but
'that Admiral Kauprianov had greater confidence
'in me and had stated that I should have the pref-
'erence. He requested me to accompany him to
'Bodega at once. We sailed down the river together
'with Captain Ringgold's boats; so it was quite an

'impressive fleet that arrived at the Bay. We
'landed at San Rafael, where we found Russian
'servants with horses ready to convey us to Bo-
'dega. Kostromitinov, as well as the captain of the
'ship *Helena*, which was lying at anchor at the
'port of Bodega, were present.

'After supper Kostromitinov made a formal
'offer on behalf of the Russian Government. He
'offered me the Russian establishment at Bodega
'and Fort Ross, together with the farms and the
'stores, as well as all the cattle and implements, and
'the schooner, aboard which the Governor had come
'to my Fort. The price for all this was extremely
'low—thirty thousand dollars with a down payment
'of two thousand dollars. The rest I was to pay in
'produce, chiefly in wheat at two dollars the
'*fanega*. No time was specified; every year the
'Russians would send down a vessel from Alaska
'and receive from me whatever quantity of wheat
'I could give them. In later years, during the gold
'rush, when I still owed some money to the Rus-
'sians, I was obliged to pay the balance in gold be-
'cause my crops had been destroyed.

'I did not hesitate to accept this favorable offer.
'The deed was drawn up immediately, written in
'French and containing the sentence, "With the
'consent of the Emperor of all Russians." Since
'the document had to be witnessed and acknowl-
'edged before an *alcalde*, we intended to go to
'Yerba Buena. Before starting on our trip across
'the Golden Gate, however, we had a grand dinner
'on board the *Helena*. Champagne flowed freely;
'we drank the health of the Russian Emperor, and
'I was toasted as the new owner of Ross and
'Bodega.

'Even before the document was signed, I was the
'acknowledged owner of all the Russian possessions
'in California. The Russians began to abandon
'their places before I started for Yerba Buena,
'some taking passage on board the *Helena*, and
'some on the *Alexander*. I wanted some of the Rus-
'sians to remain with me as hired men, but the of-
'ficers told me that they could hardly manage them
'and that I should not be able to do anything with
'them, because I was not severe enough.

'We then embarked in a small boat for Yerba

'Buena. The boat was manned by four powerful
'Russian sailors. The tide was against us, the sea
'ran high, and we narrowly escaped being drowned.
'I said to Rotchev, who accompanied me to Yerba
'Buena: "Your control over these men is so com-
'plete that they would carry you straight to hell
'if you ordered them to." However, we finally
'crossed the Golden Gate, landed safely at Yerba
'Buena and proceeded to the office of the Hudson's
'Bay Company. Here the *alcalde* joined us and
'the papers were executed. The Russians did not
'demand a note or any other document from me,
'and they continued to treat me very liberally in
'later years. With every vessel that came down the
'coast to fetch my instalment they sent supplies
'which were very necessary to me: iron, steel, am-
'munition, etc. At times I had more ammunition
'stored up than the whole California Government
'possessed. After the deed was signed by both par-
'ties, I paid over the two thousand dollars in
'money, and the transfer was complete.

'On September the twenty-eighth I sent a clerk,
'a young Englishman by the name of Robert Rid-

'ley, with a number of men to Bodega in order to
'receive the live stock. In crossing the Sacramento
'River about one hundred of the two thousand
'head of cattle were drowned. Fortunately we were
'able to save most of the hides, at that time the real
'banknotes of California. Some of the horses and
'cattle were left at Fort Ross. The schooner *Sacra-*
'*mento*, which kept up communication between
'New Helvetia and Fort Ross, brought several
'shiploads of lumber to my settlement with which
'I was enabled to finish my Fort.

'After I had bought Fort Ross, I informed the
'Mexican Government of my purchase and asked
'for a title. I was informed, however, that the Rus-
'sians had no title to the land and hence no right
'to sell it to me. If I had had a few thousand dol-
'lars of ready cash, I could have easily secured a
'legal title. Money made the Mexican authorities
'see anything. Now I regret that I did not abandon
'Fort Sutter at once in order to settle at Fort Ross.
'The location was beautiful and healthy, there was
'good soil and plenty of timber, and by far more
'improvements than at New Helvetia. There would

'have been no gold hunters to rob me; indeed, gold
'might never have been discovered.

'In the fall of 1841 and the spring of 1842, I
'gradually removed everything which I could
'carry away from Fort Ross and Bodega to Fort
'Sutter, dismantled the fort, tore down the build-
'ings, and shipped it all up on my schooner. This
'vessel of mine did me good service, and the Indians
'had become expert seamen. It was at least two
'years before I had transferred everything from
'the Russian settlements to my place, and during
'this time the schooner made numerous trips back
'and forth.

'The government not only refused to give me a
'title, but sold titles to other settlers who went to
'Ross and Bodega and took possession of my prop-
'erty. This happened mainly because Jimeno
'Casarin, Secretary of State at Monterey, was not
'very friendly toward me. If I had given him
'money, he would doubtlessly have treated me bet-
'ter. But now it happened that all the possessions
'of the Russians in California fell into the hands
'of the settlers. I never received a cent for all the

'property I was obliged to leave there. Yet I had
'made a good bargain, especially since the pay-
'ments were easy; but, as I have stated before, I
'should have left the Sacramento Valley and set-
'tled at Fort Ross.'

The bill of sale was not signed until three
months later, on the thirteenth day of December,
to be exact, before Francisco Guerrero, Justice of
Peace at Yerba Buena. Two of old California's
sturdy pioneers, Jacob Leese and Jean Vioget,
were the witnesses to the signatures. The property
thus transferred included 1700 head of cattle, 940
horses and mules, and 9000 sheep. Very welcome to
Sutter was the large variety of agricultural implements and industrial machinery so sorely
needed in the Sacramento Valley, and a considerable number of weapons. These included two brass
pieces, a number of old cannon, and a quantity of
muskets—all French weapons which had been col-
lected in the spring of 1813, after the merciless
sun had lifted the snow blanket from the path of
Napoleon's retreat from Moscow. The acquisition
of this formidable armament—formidable com-

pared to the panoply of the Californians—gave Sutter additional impetus to fortify his settlement. The conditions of the payment of the purchase price were very favorable, though not exactly as Sutter states in his narrative. He was to deliver in 1842, 1600 bushels of wheat, 160 bushels of peas, 40 bushels of beans, 50 quintales of soap, 5000 pounds of suet, 6250 pounds of tallow, the same amount in 1843, twice this amount in 1844, and $10,000 cash in 1845. It was no easy matter to collect the instalments from Sutter, and when the balance of $15,000 was finally paid over to the agent of the Russian consul in San Francisco, it was stolen. Deducting the expenses in getting the money from Sutter, the Russian American Company probably received little more than a few thousand dollars for the valuable California colonies.

VI

Political Intrigue and Foreign Influx

SUTTER had not come to California to further the
interests of a foreign power, nor had he any intention of trying to reform the rotten conditions of
the country for the benefit of natives or immigrants. His only purpose had been to build up a
fortune for himself. However, it did not take long
for him to discover that a clever and reckless man
could do better in California than merely becoming a wealthy landowner. Fate had given him all
those qualifications which are required to build up
a miniature empire of his own. With astonishing
rapidity he learned the fascinating game of po-

litical intrigue, and since he had a solid educational background and was not hampered by any patriotic inhibitions, he always had an edge on his native rivals. Even Alvarado realized finally that he had made a mistake in endowing the newcomer with such great power. But when he said that Sutter lacked delicacy, refinement, conscience, and honor, he really meant that Don Juan Agosto was a bit too shrewd and too reckless for him and his fellow compatriots.

The years before the American conquest are thus taken up by constant scheming with the various native factions, with the Hudson's Bay Company, the United States, and the French interests, always with the secret hope of becoming the Sam Houston of California. His ambition forced him at times to leave the narrow path of virtue—but then, empires are built upon selfish interest and not upon moral principles.

The bustling activities in the Sacramento Valley were sufficient to cause the *comandante general* at Sonoma sleepless nights. But worse was in store for Vallejo. In the fall of 1841 the rumor spread throughout California that Sutter was about to declare the independence of his district and seize the Sonoma frontier, and that his ally in this scheme was to be the Hudson's Bay Company.

As early as July 1840, Sutter had tried to prevent the British organization from trapping in California. He had not hesitated to accuse the Company of having designs on the territory; yet Alvarado had renewed his permission to the brigades of the Canadians to trap under certain limitations. When Sutter saw that he could not get rid of his competitors, he renewed his old friendship with the Company and tried to involve it in a plot against California. There can be no question that the commanders of the fur traders' camps had been only too willing to throw in their lot with the potentate of New Helvetia, and even Sir George Simpson, the local factor at Yerba Buena, might have made common cause with Sutter. But the clear-headed Britisher saw too well that the "Fortress of New Helvetia" could not yet afford the necessary protection for his men in case of emergency, and when he received an energetic letter from Vallejo, Sir George moved brusquely away from his supposed ally.

Sutter was not greatly chagrined by Simpson's defection. He had other trumps in his hand, and the strongest was the appearance of a French frigate to make Sutter's colony a French protectorate. J. de Rosamel, commander of the sloop *Danaide*, who came to Monterey in June 1840 to make inquiries concerning alleged mistreatment of French subjects in connection with the Graham affair, does not seem to have sought any contact with Sutter. But in September of the following year, a young dashing attaché to the French Embassy in Mexico, Eugene Duflot de Mofras, reached the Sacramento Valley on a tour of inspection. The young Frenchman was all the more impressed by the cultured, powerful Swiss because his previous visit to Vallejo had been far from pleasant. Sutter, putting up the French front of his dual Swiss nationality, with the help of young Custot made Mofras' sojourn as agreeable as possible. They led him to believe that New Helvetia was essentially a French settlement of which his government should not lose sight.

It was shortly after the Frenchman's visit that Sutter wrote a boastful letter, dated at the "Fortress of New Helvetia," November eighth, 1841, addressed to Jacob Leese, but really intended for the latter's brother-in-law, the *comandante general*. He promises to be a faithful Mexican, but any steps taken against him would lead to a declaration of independence, and the first French frigate to touch the shore of California would protect his rights. In his reminiscences Sutter prefers not to dwell upon these incidents and only gives an account of his relations to the Hudson's Bay Company.

'When I came into the valley, there were no 'other trappers in California besides those of the 'Hudson's Bay Company. Trappers from St. 'Louis never came as far as California. The trap-'ping of beaver and land otter in northern Cali-'fornia was a very profitable business; south of the 'Tulare Valley, however, hardly any furs were to

'be found. The Tulare Valley itself had once been
'a good trapping ground, but now the valley was
'better known for its abundance of wild horses.
'There were no wild horses in the Sacramento Val-
'ley, but farther south vast droves of them could
'be found. These had descended from the horses
'which the Indians had stolen from the missions.
'They increased very rapidly, especially since the
'redskins did not bother to catch them. For them it
'was easier to steal tame horses than to capture
'wild ones. In later years Americans and Cali-
'fornians caught many of these wild horses with
'lassoes. They were broken and used for breeding
'purposes.

'Every year California was visited by Hudson's
'Bay Company trappers, who left in the spring
'with a great quantity of furs. Their women were
'squaws and half-breeds who were very clever at
'making moccasins, shirts, and pantaloons of
'dressed deer skins. These were very much in de-
'mand and I bought large quantities of them.
'The company allowed their trappers to sell deer
'skins, but the sale of beaver or otter skins was

'strictly prohibited. The trappers themselves were
'chiefly Canadians, half-breeds, and Indians.

'After the Hudson's Bay Company had bought
'out the Northwest Company, it really possessed a
'monopoly of the fur trade in the entire West. The
'Company's trappers came in such large numbers
'that their camps resembled regular villages of
'pitched tents. Each group of trappers was led by
'an agent of the Company to whom the furs were
'delivered and from whom supplies were obtained.
'The name of the agent who came to the vicinity
'of New Helvetia during the first four or five years
'was La Framboise.

'I did not think that it was right that the Hud-
'son's Bay Company was allowed to carry off large
'quantities of furs every year. I also disliked the
'fact that the trappers bought stolen horses from
'the Indians. Before I came into the valley, the
'government did not have the power to stop these
'incursions. But now at my suggestion it levied a
'high export duty on furs, and trapping ceased to
'be a profitable business for the company. The

'Hudson's Bay Company, therefore, abandoned 'the valley of California, and after that there were 'no trappers in northern California except my 'own.

'Shortly after the Hudson's Bay Company was 'obliged to give up its trapping expeditions into 'California, it established a store at Yerba Buena. 'For this purpose they bought the building of 'Jacob Leese, kept a good stock of goods, and 'traded mainly in hides. Their vessels came and 'went. They brought better and cheaper goods 'than the Americans from Boston. William Glen 'Rae, who had married the daughter of Dr. John 'McLoughlin, formerly commander-in-chief of the 'Hudson's Bay Company, committed suicide in 'this building. No one knew why. He remarked to 'me one day in a fit of melancholy, "This is just 'the right weather to cut one's throat." When 'Howard and Mellus in later years erected a new 'building at the same corner, that is, the corner of 'Clay and Montgomery Streets, Rae's coffin was 'found while excavating for the foundation. After

'the discovery of gold, the Hudson's Bay Company
'wound up its affairs in California, sold its prop-
'erty, and departed for more favorable climes.'

While Sutter was plotting with the Hudson's
Bay Company and flirting with the French, he did
not lose sight of the most urgent need of attracting
immigrants into the Sacramento Valley. He needed
dependable men for his growing establishment who
could shoulder a part of the responsibilities; he
needed settlers in the valley whose fortunes would
be closely dependent on his own and who would
have to cast their lots with him in case of emergency. He succeeded remarkably well: the importance of Fort Sutter as the point at which the
foreign element converged grew from year to year.
There was hardly any pioneer of the forties who
was not, at some time or another, connected with
New Helvetia; there are few pioneer towns of any
importance in the interior valley which do not owe
their origin to one of Sutter's people.

The first men who joined him, about a year
after he had landed on the shores of the Sacramento, were two of his German companions on the

INDIAN DANCE

Drawing by Lovis Choris

FORT SUTTER

Drawing by Joseph Revere

A RIDE ALONG THE AMERICAN RIVER

Water-color drawing by E. Vischer

BEGINNINGS OF SUTTERVILLE

Lithograph by J. Cameron

overland journey: the Tyrolese Sebastian Keyser
and the Bavarian Nikolaus Allgeier. In the fall of
1841 the first organized group of emigrants, the
Bidwell-Bartleson party, crossed the Sierras into
California, and Dr. Charles Flügge, an old acquaintance from Missouri, arrived with a number
of men from the Columbia River. After that an
ever-increasing stream of home-seekers emptied
into the Sacramento Valley every fall and Fort
Sutter came to be the terminal of the great emigrant trek across the continent.

'Before I settled in the valley, it had occurred
'only once, in 1833, that a party had succeeded in
'crossing the Sierras. This was the party under
'Captain Walker, which had separated in the
'Rocky Mountains from the expedition of Captain
'Bonneville. They had struck the valley in about
'the direction of San Jose and San Juan, near
'Monterey. Some of these people had remained in
'the country, married, and settled down; others
'had returned with Walker to the Rocky Moun-
'tains. When I came into the valley, my closest
'neighbors lived more than a hundred miles dis-

[91]

'tant, Doctor John Marsh at the foot of Mount
'Diablo, and George C. Yount in the Napa Valley.
'No settler had as yet dared to move into the vast
'regions of the Sacramento and the San Joaquin
'valleys.

'The first to settle in the vicinity of the Fort was
'John Sinclair, who had been sent to California by
'Eliab Grimes, a rich merchant in the Sandwich
'Islands. In 1842 Sinclair occupied Mr. Grimes'
'grant of three leagues, the El Paso *rancho*, on
'the other side of the American River, adjoining
'my property. In the fall of the same year, I leased
'a parcel of land at the fork of the Yuba and
'Feather rivers to Theodor Cordua, who estab-
'lished the settlement of New Mecklenburg, now
'the city of Marysville; and to Nikolaus Allgeier,
'I gave without charge a piece of land of about
'two or three square miles. From this settlement by
'the Feather River, below the Bear River, de-
'veloped the town of Nicolaus. John Smith, an
'English Canadian, who settled at the Yuba near
'New Mecklenburg, and the Mexican, Pablo Gu-

'tierrez, at the Bear Creek above Nicolaus, also re-
'ceived land for nothing from me. The latter was
'killed in the revolution of 1845 and his place be-
'came known as Johnson's ranch. He carried let-
'ters from me to Micheltorena. Although the
'message was sewed up in the soles of shoes made
'expressly for the purpose, it was discovered and
'the poor fellow was hanged at San Jose. The next
'pioneers to settle on the banks of the Bear River
'were two Frenchmen, Theodore Sicard and
'Claude Chanon. Both had formerly worked for
'me, and I had given them the property known as
'the Nemshas *rancho*. On the American River,
'William Leidesdorff, a prominent business man
'of Yerba Buena, owned a grant, and on the Cos-
'umnes River were later located the farms of
'Sheldon, Daylor, Chamberlain, and Murphy.

'When I returned one day to the Fort from
'Yerba Buena, shortly after my purchase of Ross
'and Bodega, I found that the first large party of
'immigrants had arrived from Missouri. They had
'no wagons but reached the valley on horseback

'and on foot. The original party had been much
'larger, but on account of differences, several
'groups had split off. The first of these groups
'crossed into the valley at a point about opposite
'Stockton, arriving at Dr. Marsh's place on the
'fourth of November. Most of these men spent the
'winter at my settlement, and I employed as many
'as I could use. Among these was John Bidwell,
'who was to become my most faithful servant and
'partner. I liked him from the beginning, and he
'was grateful for everything I did for him and for
'his companions. Before he came to California, he
'had been a school teacher in Missouri. Just at that
'time I was badly in need of a trustworthy clerk,
'and I put him in charge of my property at Ross
'and Bodega. In the same company with Bidwell
'was Charles Weber from Hamburg, who clerked
'for me during the winter and then opened a hotel
'at San Jose. He soon acquired a little money and
'bought at a low price William Gulnac's French
'Camp *rancho* on which the city of Tuleburg, now
'Stockton, stands. Gulnac, who had a large family,
'had obtained this grant through my good office.

'Unfortunately he had taken badly to drink, and 'Weber paid the larger part of the purchase price 'in whiskey.

'Another German in Bidwell's party was Henry 'Huber. He had studied agriculture in Germany 'and was a highly educated man. I employed him 'as my superintendent of agriculture and he re-'mained with me for several years. Then he made 'a few speculations on his own which proved very 'successful. An interesting member of the party 'was Talbot H. Green, whose real name was Paul 'Geddes. He had deserted his family in Pennsyl-'vania and married the widow of Allen Montgom-'ery in California, although his first wife was still 'alive. After having made a good deal of money 'in California, he returned to Pennsylvania to live 'with his former wife, leaving his fortune, how-'ever, to the woman with whom he had lived in 'California.

'No organized emigrant party crossed the Sier-'ras in 1842, although some people came to New 'Helvetia by way of Oregon. In the following year, 'however, the large Chiles-Walker party reached

[95]

'the valley in two groups. The first group entered
'the valley farther north in the neighborhood of
'Shasta. It consisted of fourteen men among whom
'were Major Pierson Reading, Joseph Chiles,
'Samuel Hensley, Milton McGee, and four broth-
'ers Williams. They had had several hard fights
'with the Indians; McGee had fallen into a bear
'trap during one of these fights. When these men
'came to the Fort, I again placed a number of
'them in my employment. Reading became my
'bookkeeper and Hensley I made super-cargo of
'the schooner and superintendent of my business
'at the Bay.

'The second group entered the valley south of
'Stockton. They had likewise been obliged to aban-
'don their wagons, and Chiles went down to assist
'them. There were several women in this party,
'among them the two daughters of George Yount,
'one of whom later on married John Davis, an
'English blacksmith. After the latter had killed
'himself at Yerba Buena, she became the wife of
'Eugene Sullivan, and subsequently the mother-in-
'law of Senator Jones.

'After that immigration continued in small par-
'ties. They were usually just strong enough to pro-
'tect themselves against the hostile Indians. All
'immigrants were hospitably received by me. I took
'into my service as many as I could, and others
'could stay under my roof as long as they liked.
'When they left me, I provided them with pass-
'ports which were respected everywhere. All build-
'ings and houses of my settlement were filled every
'winter with wet, poor, and hungry immigrants—
'men, women, and children. Sometimes the houses
'were so full of people, that I could hardly find a
'place to sleep. Most immigrants arrived in a desti-
'tute condition, very few had saved their teams,
'and some had lost everything on their long jour-
'ney across the continent. Often I had to go with
'my men to pull them out of the snow, and I was
'able to save many lives in this way.

'A terrible catastrophe occurred in the fall of
'1846. One day a young man by the name of
'Charles Stanton appeared at my Fort and re-
'ported that a large group of immigrants, the
'Donner Party, was in distress. I furnished Mr.

'Stanton with a horse and dispatched two mounted
'Indian boys with seven pack mules heavily loaded
'with provisions. Since the company had in the
'meantime lost everything, the provisions were by
'far not sufficient, and the starving sufferers killed
'first the mules, then the horses, and finally, even
'my good Indians. These Indians had tried to
'cross the Sierras together with the so-called "For-
'lorn Hope," a group of men and women making a
'desperate attempt to break through the snow.
'When they heard that the white men talked about
'killing them, they escaped during the night; next
'day, however, they were caught while scratching
'the snow for acorns, whereupon the white men
'killed and devoured them. The four relief parties
'which left the Fort during the winter succeeded in
'saving about half of the number of the ill-fated
'travelers.

'I did not have much trouble with the immi-
'grants until after the discovery of gold. To be
'sure, there were always people who complained;
'some said that the best land was already occupied
'and others who happened to arrive in the dry sea-

'son thought that the valley was no fit place in 'which to live and went on to the coast. But other-'wise the newcomers were grateful for everything 'I did for them.'

On March sixth, 1844, there arrived for the first time at New Helvetia a man who was to play a decisive rôle in the future history of California: John Charles Frémont. He and his party were engaged in the second of his western explorations; they had come south from the Klamath River and had crossed the mountains under the greatest difficulties. "When we arrived at the Fort," reports Frémont's guide Kit Carson, "we were as naked and in as poor a condition as men possibly could be. We were well received by Mr. Sutter and furnished in a princely manner everything we required." For Sutter, however, this and the future visits of the famous soldier and explorer meant nothing but annoyance and embarrassment.

'While I was walking outside of the gate one 'evening, two horsemen rode up and saluted me. 'They at once took me for the owner of the Fort. 'Noticing that they were wearing Scotch caps, I

'asked them if they belonged to the Hudson's Bay
'Company. One of them replied laughingly: "I
'know why you ask this question," and then in-
'troduced himself as John Frémont, an officer of
'the United States Government. His companion
'was Kit Carson, who had conducted him across
'the desert and the mountains.

'Frémont was the leader of an expedition of the
'Topographical Bureau at Washington, engaged
'in exploring the country west of the Rocky Moun-
'tains. At the upper American River the party had
'been obliged to give up its journey because of lack
'of provisions. Frémont, who had heard of my set-
'tlement and knew the general direction, had set
'out with Kit Carson to find assistance. I ordered
'a *vaquero* to take their horses and invited them in.
'Carson returned immediately to the camp with the
'supplies which I gave them, while Frémont stayed
'with me over-night. They camped in the vicinity
'of my Fort for about three weeks. I gave Frémont
'everything he wanted, and what I did not have
'was fetched from Yerba Buena by my schooner.
'I sold him thirty horses, eighty mules, a number

'of fat cattle, clothing, provisions, saddles, etc. I
'charged everything at cost and accepted orders on
'the Topographical Bureau. No one in California
'would have given Frémont a dollar of credit and I
'was obliged to sell these orders at a discount of
'twenty per cent. In the innocence of my heart I
'thought I would do the American Government a
'favor by not taking advantage of Frémont's dis-
'tress, but I only cheated myself thereby.

'All of Frémont's animals had to be shoed at my
'blacksmith shop, and a number of riding as well
'as pack saddles had to be made in my saddlery.
'Frémont accused three of his men of stealing
'sugar. They were tried before me and I found
'them not guilty. Frémont did not like my de-
'cision and discharged the three men. These men
'were very glad to leave him, and I was glad to
'give them employment. One of them was Samuel
'Neal, a good blacksmith, who in later years be-
'came a very rich man and a well-known breeder of
'Holsteins. On the twenty-fourth of March the
'party left for the Kern River, whence they in-
'tended to return to the United States.

'As an official of the Government it was my duty 'to report the Captain's arrival. The Governor 'dispatched Lieutenant-Colonel Rafael Tellez, 'afterwards governor of Sinaloa, with a captain, 'a lieutenant, and twenty-five dragoons to inquire 'about Captain Frémont's business in California. 'Since I had sent in my report rather late, Tellez 'did not arrive at New Helvetia before March 'twenty-seventh, when Frémont was already well 'on his way.

'While thus many a stranger arrived at my Fort 'and was befriended by me, I did not dare to have 'my family come to California until many years 'later. When I embarked for America, I left my 'family, consisting of Mrs. Sutter and five chil-'dren, four sons, the youngest of whom died in '1834, and one daughter, in Switzerland. After I 'left Missouri, I did not hear from them for two or 'three years, for I had to write to my wife first, 'where and which way to send her letters. After I 'had settled in California, my letters were first dis-'patched through the Hudson's Bay Company, 'which conducted a regular express service over

'the Rocky Mountains to Canada with fifty
'armed men. Later I sent some letters to Sitka,
'from where the Russian mail service brought them
'to St. Petersburg by way of Kamchatka and Si-
'beria. Either way it took about a year before my
'letters reached my family. My children received a
'good education in Switzerland and reached Cali-
'fornia safely with their mother in 1849.'

VII

Alliance with Micheltorena

THE activities of Sutter and the growing influence of his colony were among the principal reasons which brought about Vallejo's decision to send an emissary to the central government in Mexico. This messenger, Victor Prudon, was instructed by the *comandante general* to call the government's attention to the serious danger which threatened Mexican sovereignty by the foreign element. Vallejo suggested the appointment of a new governor who should unite civil and military authority in his hands and should be supported by a strong disciplined troop of Mexican soldiers. When Pru-

don arrived in Mexico City during the last days of
February, 1842, together with two representatives
of Alvarado sent on a similar mission, they found
to their surprise that Santa Ana, the new president, had already anticipated Vallejo's suggestion.
On the twenty-second of January, Manuel Micheltorena had been appointed governor, inspector,
and *comandante general* of California.

The new Governor disembarked at San Diego on
the twenty-fifth of August, 1842, but officially did
not enter upon his duties until the first of the following January. At first, it appeared as if he
would understand how to gain the confidence of
natives and foreigners alike. But since he did not
possess the necessary qualities to put the affairs of
California in order, it was easy for the Alvarado-
Castro party to arouse the provincial sentiment
against the Mexican general. Moreover, the *batallón fijo de Californias*, which had accompanied
him from Mexico, consisted partly of released con-
victs who turned out to be a constant source of embarrassment to the Governor and a regular
infliction upon the citizens of the territory.

In the turbulent days of Micheltorena's reign, which culminated in the deportation of the General together with his convict soldiers, the Lord of New Helvetia was to play an important, though not very enviable rôle.

'Even before Micheltorena's arrival in Cali-'fornia he had been prejudiced against me by Vic-'tor Prudon, whom Vallejo had sent to Mexico. 'Prudon had informed Micheltorena that I had 'built a strong fort, which was the nucleus of the 'dangerous foreign element, and that I had 'threatened to make a second Texas of California, 'if the Mexican Government should make an at-'tempt to interfere with my plan of settlement. 'Vallejo had solicited troops from Mexico to put 'me down, and in answer to these solicitations, 'Micheltorena had come with Prudon and several 'hundred soldiers.

'Believing that Micheltorena was wrongly in-'formed about my intentions, I sent William 'Flügge to him. Mr. Flügge was a German lawyer 'and a very able diplomatist, who knew several lan-'guages and was extremely courteous in dealings

'with other people. I had become acquainted with
'him in St. Louis, and just now he was at the Fort
'as my guest; later he was in my employ as secre-
'tary and legal adviser. Flügge met Micheltorena
'at Los Angeles where the Governor resided dur-
'ing the first months of his reign. He explained to
'him that I had no evil intentions against the
'Mexican Government and that I only resented en-
'croachments from the Californians. The latter
'were constantly interfering with my business, and
'General Vallejo in particular had repeatedly
'thrown obstacles in the way of my communica-
'tions with the Bay. He required a passport of my
'men passing through Sonoma on their way from
'Sacramento to Fort Ross, and when the cattle
'were driven from the Russian settlements, they
'had to be taken by way of Sonoma for a close ex-
'amination, to determine whether there were not
'any animals among them belonging to Vallejo or
'his neighbors. I was finally obliged to get a pass
'from the government at Monterey which made
'me independent of Vallejo. This only added fuel
'to the anger of the latter.

'The new Governor appeared satisfied with
'Flügge's representations. He wrote me a very
'kind letter, stating that he had nothing against
'me. In the fall of 1844 he invited me to visit him
'at Monterey. I was naturally very anxious to ac-
'cept this invitation and went to Monterey accom-
'panied by Major Bidwell and a number of armed
'men. On my way to the capital I visited James
'Forbes, the British vice-consul, at his residence
'near San Jose. Forbes, having married a daugh-
'ter of the country, was naturally in the secrets of
'the Californians and knew everything that was
'going on. He told me that the native Californians
'were preparing to attack Micheltorena and send
'him and his troops out of the country. They did
'not want Mexican cut-throats to stand guard over
'them. As a matter of fact, the revolutionists were
'ready to blockade the General at Monterey, to
'send him back to Mexico, and to select a new gov-
'ernor from their own people. Captain Jean Vioget
'had been engaged by Castro and Alvarado to be
'ready with his vessel to embark with the Mexicans.
'I was well aware of what we could expect if the

'Californians were to succeed in their scheme.
'They would soon drive us foreigners out of the
'country as they had attempted once before in the
'winter of 1840.

'At Monterey I was received with greatest civil
'and military honors. Micheltorena arranged a
'great dinner in my honor. After the banquet the
'Governor and I, as captain of the Mexican militia,
'reviewed the garrison lined up in parade, and in
'the evening a large balloon was sent up into the
'sky.

'I remained in Monterey several days and saw
'Micheltorena every day. It was quite natural that
'I informed him of the plot which the Californians
'were hatching. This was the first he had heard of
'it and he was very glad that I had told him about
'it. He said that he would be on his guard and com-
'plained that the Californians treated him badly,
'although he had had the best of intentions. The
'Governor immediately called a council of war at
'which I was present. I entered into a compact with
'him to render him every military assistance when-
'ever he would call for it. I received orders to raise

'as strong an auxiliary force as I possibly could
'and to be ready to march upon the receipt of the
'Governor's orders. Micheltorena on his part
'agreed to give me and all other settlers in the val-
'ley titles to our lands and to bear all expenses con-
'nected with the campaign. As a result of our ne-
'gotiations, he sent me what was called a "general
'title," signed at Monterey on the twenty-second of
'December, copies of which I sent to those who had
'applied for land grants. Upon the Governor's in-
'structions I made out deeds, which were later de-
'clared void. Since these titles were legal, the
'courts should have recognized them.

'I had intended to embark for Yerba Buena on
'board the *Sterling*, a Boston trader. However, I
'was detained on board the frigate *Savannah*, an
'American man-of-war lying at anchor in the har-
'bor at Monterey. In the meantime the *Sterling* set
'sail with my luggage, and I endeavored in vain
'to overtake her with a small boat. Therefore, I re-
'turned to the *Savannah*, spent the night on board
'this vessel, and the next morning I took passage

'for Yerba Buena with the *Don Quixote*. My
'schooner was waiting in the harbor of Yerba
'Buena, and after I had given orders to transfer
'my luggage from the *Sterling*, I hastened to the
'customs house to greet the Mexican officers. I did
'not lose any time in getting back on board my
'ship, for I was afraid that the news of my friendly
'relations with the Governor might have in the
'meantime reached the ears of those who were on
'the point of declaring war on him. As I heard
'later on, Castro, expecting me to return overland,
'had lain in ambush for me at San Juan. When he
'found out that his plan was thwarted, he sent
'orders to Yerba Buena for my arrest, but by the
'time the messenger arrived, I was safely on my
'way to Sacramento.

'When I reached New Helvetia, I immediately
'began preparations for the expected campaign. I
'organized and drilled companies, and my Fort
'had all the appearances of a military camp. All
'the settlers in the valley were enthusiastic for the
'cause and joined me heartily. Only Sinclair, whom

'I had made my aide-de-camp, and Cordua, who 'served in the ranks, acted cowardly and backed 'out soon after we had started.'

Alas, Cordua and Sinclair were not the only settlers who looked upon Sutter's enterprise with mixed feelings. Not only were the citizens of central and southern California either neutral or on the side of Alvarado and Castro, many foreigners in the north considered the whole affair as one to be fought out by the Californians themselves, and this in spite of the glowing promises of land grants which Micheltorena had made. But all attempts to dissuade Sutter from arming foreigners and Indians and from joining Micheltorena's vagabonds were bound to be fruitless. He turned a deaf ear to the warnings which Vallejo gave him in a long, friendly letter of December eighteenth, as well as to a more direct remonstrance from José Castro a few days later. When Charles Weber arrived at New Helvetia around Christmas to have a heart-to-heart talk with Sutter in their native German, he was promptly arrested and kept in jail until the end of the campaign. The same fate threatened

Dr. John Marsh when he first refused the order
of the "Commander-in-Chief of the Forces of the
Rio Sacramento" to join his ranks. Sutter took
great delight in forcing the grouchy doctor to
march in the company of infantry as a common
soldier—much to his own regret, as the Captain
was soon to find out.

'At the end of December I received marching
'orders from the Governor. On the first day of
'1845 we left the Fort with music and flying colors
'for Doctor Marsh's farm near *Monte Diablo*.
'My force consisted of several hundred men: a
'company of eighty-five riflemen under Captain
'John Gantt, a former officer of the United States
'army; a company of over one hundred Indians,
'well drilled and commanded in German by Ernst
'Rufus, with Jacob Dür and Rufino, the Chief of
'the Mokelumnes, as lieutenants; a small squadron
'of cavalry, native Californians who had deserted
'Vallejo and joined me; and a detachment of artil-
'lery. In the Fort I left a garrison of about fifteen
'white men and thirty Indian sharpshooters in
'command of Major Reading. The cavalry and

[113]

'artillery took the land route, while the infantry
'was embarked on my schooner. We all met at *Los
'Meganos.*

'Doctor Marsh was opposed to us. As he feared,
'however, that I would arrest him, he joined me
'and marched as a common soldier in the ranks.
'But he remained a traitor. The next day we set
'out toward San Jose Mission. Here the cavalry
'caught a spy who had been sent from Castro's
'headquarters at San Jose to reconnoiter and re-
'port. I had the man brought before me, but he
'gave evasive answers to my questions. Although I
'had him put under guard, he succeeded in making
'his escape. My corporal jumped upon an unsad-
'dled horse, caught the spy with a lasso and
'brought him back. I ordered him to be hand-
'cuffed, but told him that I should release him as
'soon as he reached his home near San Jose.

'The whole country stood in awe of me. Such a
'military force had never before been seen in this
'part of the world. Early the next morning I dis-
'patched a vanguard of twenty-five mounted rifle-
'men to the Mission of San Jose and then followed

'with my entire force. With my staff I went to the
'mission's padre, who received us very kindly. The
'inhabitants of the missions were all Mexicans, and
'therefore on our side. We were told that Castro
'had commenced to fortify himself at the mission
'but had not expected that we would arrive at the
'place so soon. He had fled with the entire garrison
'upon the news of our approach, and the padre be-
'lieved that he had gone to Santa Clara. We had
'ample refreshments served to us, but some of my
'men could not resist drinking too much of the
'wine which the *major domo* placed before them,
'and they became intoxicated. I decided, therefore,
'that it would be best to continue our march as
'soon as possible. We started immediately on the
'road to the *Pueblo de San Jose* and camped that
'night within five miles of the town.

'We kept strict guard because Castro was sup-
'posed to be not far off with a considerable force.
'In addition to the provisions which the padre had
'sent to me I had two oxen killed for my men that
'night. Before we set out the next morning, I sent
'orders to the *alcalde* to close all places where

'liquor was sold. I knew that I had some bad cus-
'tomers among my riflemen. Toward noon we en-
'tered San Jose. With an escort of twenty-five men
'I went to the house of Antonio Suñol, an old
'Spaniard, who told me that the *alcalde*, Antonio
'Mario Pico, had become frightened at my ap-
'proach and had fled with almost the entire male
'population. Suñol expressed the opinion that
'Castro had left Santa Clara with all his men and
'had joined the main force, which was blockading
'Micheltorena at Monterey. Then we marched
'through the city of San Jose and continued our
'course southward.

'The second night after having left San Jose we
'camped at San Juan. Monterey had been be-
'sieged, but the day before our arrival the siege
'had been raised and the insurgents had fled to-
'ward the South. Leaving a strong force as a gar-
'rison, Micheltorena marched out of Monterey
'with several hundred men and joined me at the
'Salinas River. We then arranged the order of
'march. The whole force was divided into two di-
'visions, the Governor commanding one, and I the

'other. I was made a colonel, and a squadron of 'dragoons with a trumpeter was put at my dis-'posal.

'Every evening after our day's march, the 'quartermaster laid out the camp, the tents were 'pitched, the necessary orders and the watch-word 'for the night were given. The Mexican soldiers 'often wanted to tear down the fences of firewood, 'but I forbade them to do that and sent them to 'the distant forests for firewood. They obeyed me, 'and Micheltorena's officers marveled that the men 'executed my orders so well. The two divisions al-'ways camped near to one another, and Michel-'torena and I exchanged visits. This showed that 'he respected me as being on equal terms with him.

'One night we stopped at the Mission San Luis 'Obispo, and a few days later we were quartered in 'the buildings at the Mission Santa Ynez. From 'this point we had to build a road for the cannon 'along the beach to Santa Barbara. This occa-'sioned a delay of several days, during which time 'we enjoyed the excellent meals and good quarters 'at the mission. At Santa Barbara we likewise

'found good quarters at the mission and were well
'received by the bishop and three of the priests.

'Captain Wilson invited me and a few of my of-
'ficers to have supper with him. While we were eat-
'ing, the captain of cavalry, Santiago Estrada,
'came in and called me to one side. He told me that
'Governor Micheltorena had sent him with a guard
'of twenty-five men for my protection, as he had
'received information which made him fearful lest
'I should be seized and made prisoner. I told Es-
'trada that I would make some excuse and go with
'him as soon as possible. A short time later we all
'left Captain Wilson's hospitable house and were
'escorted by Estrada to headquarters. Michel-
'torena was then sick with piles. He could not
'mount his horse but was obliged to travel in a
'kind of buggy in which he could stretch himself
'at full length. I found him in bed when I returned
'from Captain Wilson's, and he said that he be-
'lieved I had been in danger.

'The next day the padres invited us to have
'breakfast with them at the mission. When we left,
'the bishop gave me his benediction. While the

'army marched to El Rincon, I remained with a
'guard of twenty-five men in Santa Barbara in
'order to get necessary articles. First I went to
'Captain Wilson's store where his stepson, the
'later governor, Romualdo Pacheco, then a lad of
'about seventeen, was a clerk. I ordered a hundred
'pairs of pants for my soldiers, but he had only
'seventy pairs of duck trousers. I also bought
'shirts, tobacco, and other articles from him and
'from other merchants. The orders which I gave
'them in return for these things were afterwards
'all paid. I procured horses and everything else
'that I required in this same way. I would not per-
'mit my soldiers to plunder, and did everything
'in my power to protect the property.

'At El Rincon we camped several days in wet
'weather. We did not have much meat, but my
'Indians gathered quantities of mussels and clams.
'A great many soldiers of my division deserted. A
'number of men of the mounted rifles, the detach-
'ment of California cavalry, joined their country-
'men, the rebels, as did many of the Mexican dra-
'goons. Castro was at this time encamped at Buena

'Ventura, about twenty or twenty-five miles dis-
'tant. James Coates, a lieutenant in the rifle com-
'pany, was sent forward with a patrol to recon-
'noiter. He set out by way of the beach and re-
'turned the next day with the report that all had
'been captured. He told us that they were treated
'well and had been released upon their word not to
'take up arms again against the Californians. I
'had my doubts as to the trustworthiness of this
'story, but we were obliged to let them go.

'It was now decided to attack the enemy, and I
'was appointed to lead the attack. With my entire
'command, enforced by the Mexican dragoons and
'by two companies of Mexican infantry, all in all
'about six hundred men, I started about sundown
'to cross the mountain range. Micheltorena with
'the artillery and the remainder of the army
'waited until the next morning to continue the
'march along the beach.

'During the night it rained very hard. The hills
'became slippery, men and horses fell and rolled
'down into the ravines. When day broke, I found
'myself in the forest in sight of the Mission Buena

'Ventura, but not more than half of my command
'had come up. A council of war was held. Captain
'Gantt believed that not half of the guns would
'go off, and Lieutenant Felix Valdes did not think
'that we were strong enough to make the attack.
'Estrada likewise considered an attack in broad
'daylight as inadvisable, since we had not arrived
'in time for a night attack. Only the captain of the
'Indian company, Ernst Rufus, now a farmer in
'the neighborhood of Sonoma, was confident, and
'said that the muskets of his company were in
'order, for his Indians had taken good care of
'them.

'In the meanwhile stragglers kept on coming up
'and we were gradually getting stronger. I told my
'officers that an immediate attack might have good
'results, since the enemy would hardly expect us in
'such weather. Furthermore, I had been informed
'that they had had a *fandango* the night before
'and were probably still half drunk and asleep. At
'all events, I was determined to make the attack.
'Taking with me as many men as I could gather, I
'made a charge upon the town. The merry-makers

'of yesterday were panic-stricken and fled in every
'direction. Since we came out of the woods, they
'could not tell how strong we were; hence they did
'not stop running until they came to an open place
'about three-quarters of a mile away where they
'tried to form ranks. They began to swear at us,
'as was their fashion, calling us thieves and all
'kinds of bad names.

'I sent Bidwell back to Micheltorena to ask for
'permission to pursue the enemy. But the Gover-
'nor believed that it would be better to continue the
'march together. If we had followed up our ad-
'vantage, we could have easily routed them, but
'this would not have been according to the Mex-
'ican military tradition. First of all we had to eat
'and to drink now. In accordance with the orders
'of the Governor, who in the meantime had come
'up and entered the town, I demanded wine, *aguar-*
'*diente,* and meat from the *major domo.* While the
'priest of the mission was on our side, the *major*
'*domo* favored the enemy. He protested against my
'requisitions, pretending that Castro and his men
'had taken away everything. Since I was convinced

'that this was not true, I threatened to break open
'his cellar if he would not produce the provisions
'which I required. When he saw me determined, he
'yielded at length and provided plenty of every-
'thing. We spent all next day at the mission, eat-
'ing and drinking well and enjoying the dances of
'the long-haired and short-shirted Indians from
'the Mission San Antonio, who had come to play
'for us. The Indians had a regular band with them.
'The inhabitants of the mission informed me that
'the Californians had threatened to nail me to a
'large cross at the mission if they could catch me.'

VIII

The "Battle of Cahuenga" and Its Sad Results.

THE history of military strategy shows numerous examples of gradually diminishing fighting power during a long, continuous offensive. With 450,000 men Napoleon crossed the Russian frontier in the spring of 1812; only 50,000 arrived at the gates of Moscow. The Army of the Potomac, 122,000 strong, left the Rapidan in May 1864; little more than half of that number assembled six weeks later at City Point. Of the "army" that marched from New Helvetia on the first of January, hardly 150 warriors arrived at El Rincon, and probably not more than a few dozens, outside of the well dis-

[124]

ciplined Indian detachment, took part in the "Grand Battle of Cahuenga" on the twentieth of February.

The "battle" itself, which brought this Don Quixotic campaign to an inglorious finish, was fought strictly in accordance with the well-tried principle of California warfare: "Don't hurt me, and I won't hurt you!" Although a roaring cannonade was kept up all afternoon, causing the panic-stricken women of Los Angeles to assemble on the highest elevation in heart-rending prayers, the only casualties were one cannon wheel smashed and a horse's head blown off—or a tail, according to equally reliable sources. Sutter, like all Swiss a lover of military display, gives the most detailed though hardly the most reliable account of this bloodless affair. Whether his capture by the Californians was as accidental as he presents it in his memoirs will remain an unanswered question.

'Then we continued our march and came close 'to the enemy again. Several times during the 'night Castro's men succeeded in stealing horses 'from us.

'As we passed the Santa Clara farm on our
'march, a beautiful woman, said to have been the
'mistress of former Governor Alvarado, was wait-
'ing for us. A boy at her side, who was supposed
'to be her son, carried a stack of *tortillas* wrapped
'in a cloth. The couple approached the soldiers and
'inquired about the captain of the riflemen. When
'Captain Gantt was pointed out to them, the boy
'presented him with the package. Within the bun-
'dle Captain Gantt found a letter signed by
'Castro, Alvarado, and others, calling upon him
'and his company to abandon Micheltorena and go
'over to the other side. Gantt showed me the letter
'immediately, and I in turn handed it to the Gov-
'ernor. That evening we camped in a large vine-
'yard surrounded by a stone wall in which our
'horses were safe. I did not sleep at all. I had to be
'constantly on the lookout for the enemy, who did
'all in its power to harass us. The Governor was
'still sick in bed, and the whole responsibility
'rested on my shoulders. A woman, the mother of
'thirteen children, came to me and begged me not

'to be hard on her nine sons who were serving in
'Castro's force.

'The next night we camped at Cahuenga, an
'adobe belonging to the Mission San Fernando.
'From the hill close by we could see the camp of
'the enemy. The wind was blowing very hard and
'we were fearfully annoyed by the flying sand and
'dust. During the night our tents were blown down
'by the wind. We kept a strong guard and nearly
'everybody was awake. At daylight we prepared
'for the attack. The fife, the bass drum, and three
'small drums, belonging to my own company, gave
'the signal. The firing of the cannon on both sides
'gave proof that the conflict was about to begin.
'About sunrise we began to march against the
'enemy, the cannon and the infantry in front and
'the cavalry on the two flanks. Micheltorena was
'mounted and in the field. He had command of
'the artillery and the infantry, and I commanded
'the cavalry. Firing commenced on both sides. The
'first shot from our cannon broke the wheel of one
'of their field pieces. The enemy became fright-

'ened and those in charge of the cannon took to
'their heels. Had we rushed upon them immedi-
'ately, we might have secured the victory.

'But we had bad luck. Some of the Mexican
'dragoons who were with us began to waver and a
'number of them deserted. The order to charge was
'not obeyed by the riflemen. I saw treachery lurk-
'ing behind guns and said to Micheltorena: "I
'shall go and see why Gantt does not advance."
'To my great surprise, I found his men casting a
'ballot to determine whether they should stay on
'our side or go over to the enemy. The Americans
'in our ranks said that they would not fight
'against the Americans on the other side. More-
'over, Castro had received reënforcements from
'San Diego, and our men began to get frightened.
'Doctor Marsh, who was there as a private, was a
'good talker and knew how to stir up mutiny.

'I said sharply to Gantt: "What do you mean
'by not obeying orders? Why do you not ad-
'vance?"

'He replied insolently: "We are voting to see

'who wants to stay on this side and who wants
'to go over to the other side."

' "This is the time to fight and not to vote," I
'replied angrily.

'At this point about thirty Americans, who had
'only recently crossed over the mountains into
'California, together with settlers from Los An-
'geles, came over to our side and tried to persuade
'our men not to continue the attack. We told them
'that they were foolish, that Micheltorena was the
'friend of the settlers, and that those who wanted
'land should fight for him. But the others had a
'different story to tell and caused delay and dis-
'satisfaction.

'When I became convinced that I could not do
'anything with Gantt and when I saw that a good
'many Californians were coming over to our side,
'I determined to make my way back to Michel-
'torena. The Governor had been fighting well all
'this time and had gained a position on a wooded
'hill. He defended himself on this hill until evening
'and then camped there.

'On my way back to Micheltorena I suddenly
'found myself surrounded by thirty Californians.
'Had they known who I was, they would doubtless
'have cut me to pieces. Luckily Antonio Castro
'came up, and recognizing me, said to the men: "I
'shall take over your prisoner." He then saluted
'me and said: "I am very glad that you are here."

' "Yes," said I, "but I am not."

'Then he said that he would send for Alvarado,
'and dispatched a *vaquero*. Alvarado came after
'a short while, dismounted, and embraced me like
'an old friend. Alvarado then ordered his *vaquero*
'to give him the bottle and we all had a good drink
'of *aguardiente*. Then he sent a *vaquero* for José
'Castro, who appeared presently. "Castro," said
'Alvarado to him, "dismount and salute Captain
'Sutter." We dismounted and embraced each
'other. Then we all got into the saddle again and
'rode to the adobe at Cahuenga. I rode between
'Castro and Alvarado, and the mounted Califor-
'nians, who looked as though they would like to
'eat me up, formed a hollow square around us. At
'Cahuenga I was incarcerated in a dark room. My

'double rifle, a splendid little weapon, had to be
'left in front of the door and it was soon gone
'forever.

'While I was in my cell, many curious men and
'women came to look at me as if I were a strange
'animal. An officer entered with a strong guard
'and demanded my sword. As I handed it to him,
'I thought to myself that things really looked dark
'for me. Fortunately I saw an officer by the name
'of Eugenio Montenegro, a captain of cavalry,
'whom I knew very well. I beckoned to him and
'said: "You can do me a great favor. Tell your
'superiors that they know nothing of the usages
'of war, if they put an officer of my rank under
'a common guard." This had the desired effect.
'My sword was given back to me, I was invited
'into another room where the officers were drinking
'and was asked to join them. They told me that
'they needed all their men and would send me to
'Los Angeles accompanied by the *alcalde*, Antonio
'Lugo. John Rowland, a wealthy farmer from Los
'Angeles, happened to be present and gave his
'word as security that I would not escape. So in

[131]

'the evening I was taken to Los Angeles, about
'twelve miles distant, by the *alcalde* and Mr. Row-
'land.

'In Los Angeles I was quartered in the house
'of Abel Stearns. In the same house the officers of
'the new government, that is, the government
'formed by the Castro party, the rebel govern-
'ment, as we called it, had gathered to celebrate the
'victory by a banquet. Pio Pico, the new Governor,
'was not present that night, but Juan Bandini,
'the Secretary of State, and all the others were
'there. They invited me to sit down at the table
'with them. I declined because I had just come
'from the battlefield and was dirty and jaded.
'When they insisted, I sat down with them but told
'them after a short while that I was tired and
'asked them to excuse me. Mr. Stearns took me to
'a good room. There were no women in the town
'at that time; all had taken flight. Later when I
'was presented to some of the ladies, I laughed and
'asked if they had thought that we would kill them.
'They replied: "You had bad Mexicans and
'Indians with you."

[132]

'During the night Mr. Stearns came to my door,
'and after knocking repeatedly, he finally aroused
'me. I was so worn out that I could shake off the
'sleep only with great difficulty. Mr. Stearns told
'me that two gentlemen had arrived and wished to
'see me. When I had dressed and come out of my
'room, I found Andres Pico, captain of militia
'at Los Angeles, and James McKinley, a Scotch-
'man. They wanted me to write to Micheltorena,
'advising him to yield because it was fruitless to
'resist any longer and because it would be more
'prudent to surrender at once.

'Although I was convinced that they were
'speaking the truth and that there was no hope for
'our cause, I did not like to give Micheltorena my
'advice. I wanted him to do as he pleased. They
'also wished me to write to Rufus, the captain of
'the Indians. As an excuse I told them that I could
'not write Spanish and that Rufus could under-
'stand nothing but German. To Micheltorena I
'could write in French, I told them. "But," they
'said, "we can read neither French nor German."
' "You surely have some one who can," I replied.

'It was in the middle of the night, however, and 'I was satisfied that they would not examine too 'closely what I said. So I wrote to Micheltorena in 'French in such a manner that he would under-'stand my position and would know that I was 'forced to write. After this interruption I slept 'soundly until morning.

'Micheltorena was by this time entirely sur-'rounded by the enemy, and his provisions could 'not have lasted more than a day or two. He might, 'of course, have retired and fought a little longer, 'but his men were deserting him in large numbers, 'and there was no hope for a victorious outcome. 'He surrendered the next day.

'The news of Micheltorena's capitulation was 'brought to me in the forenoon of the following 'day by the French surgeon, Dr. Alfred Anselin. 'The doctor, who had formerly been in my employ 'and then physician of the *batallón fijo*, remarked 'gravely: "I have other bad news for you."

' "What is it?" said I.

' "There is much discussion going on as to what 'shall be done with you," he replied. "Some are 'for shooting you, others for deportation and 'confiscation of all your property."

' "I am in their power," I said; "they can do 'with me as they please."

'After Doctor Anselin had left me, the brother 'of my clerk Juan Vaca came and brought a clean 'shirt and a razor. I was very glad of this because 'all my luggage had been left behind at San Fer- 'nando where Doctor John Townsend, my aide-de- 'camp, had taken charge of it.

'After the surrender a great many soldiers 'streamed into Los Angeles. With the capitulation 'they were free to do what they pleased. Michel- 'torena had received permission to march through 'Los Angeles with music and flying colors. This 'music sounded like a funeral march to me. I was 'really the greatest sufferer. Defeat meant much 'more to me than to the Governor. After the march 'his men had to ground their arms. Micheltorena 'himself was allowed to return to Monterey and 'settle his affairs before leaving the country. 'Among those who had laid down their arms were 'my Indians. In the capitulation they had been

'given every advantage which the Mexican soldiers
'had received, but they were badly treated while
'I was held prisoner. They were obliged to carry
'burdens from Los Angeles to San Pedro like pack
'animals to supply provisions for the vessels on
'which the Mexican soldiers were to be sent home.
'For this they received no pay and scarcely enough
'food to keep them alive.

'John Bidwell called on me the next morning
'and brought me some oranges. He was then as
'always my most faithful assistant. Since I was
'not allowed to leave the house, Bidwell and an
'Englishman by the name of James Smith break-
'fasted with me in my room.

'The next day permission was granted to me, on
'my parole, to visit the Frenchman, Jean Vignes,
'one of the richest men in Los Angeles, whose house
'was only a few hundred yards from Mr. Stearns'
'place. There I met José Valdes and a few other
'Mexican officers. Vignes treated us all with some
'excellent wine. I returned to my quarters for din-
'ner, and after the meal, Bandini called and invited
'me for a walk in the garden. He offered me a

'cigar and asked me to play a game of billiards
'with him. He was one of the few men in the coun-
'try who owned a billiard table. I asked him to
'excuse me since I was in no humor to play bil-
'liards.

'"Yes," he replied, "I believe you." Then he
'continued: "But now tell me, please, what made
'you throw your lot with Micheltorena? Did you
join him of your own free will, or did you receive
'orders to march?"

'I told him that I had received orders from the
'Governor to march.

'"Have you these orders?" said he. "Can you
'show them to me?"

'"I had them with me," I told him, "and I be-
'lieve that they are with my baggage at San
'Fernando. I believe that I could get the papers
'if I had horses to send my servants to San
'Fernando."

'He said that it would be very difficult to pro-
'cure horses, but finally I succeeded in sending a
'messenger to San Fernando. Doctor Townsend
'came and brought my papers, among which was

[137]

'Micheltorena's marching order for me. I imme-
'diately handed over the order to Bandini, who
'exclaimed after he had read it: "Now you are
'saved!" He took my papers to the government
'house and showed them to Pio Pico, to Castro, and
'to all other officials who happened to be there.
'Bandini, who was a native of Peru and an edu-
'cated man, tried to do everything to give my
'affairs a favorable turn. The next day after
'breakfast he called for me and accompanied me to
'the government building. Pico, Castro, Alvarado,
'and the other officials of the new government were
'assembled and expected me. They told me that
'they had become convinced that I had done noth-
'ing but my duty to the former legal government.
'They would recognize my position and reinstate
'me in all my former rights if I would promise to
'serve the new government as faithfully as I had
'served Micheltorena. I was to retain all my prop-
'erty and my offices. These offices were *comandante*
'*militar de las fronteras del norte y encargado de*
'*la justicia,* the former title having been conferred
'on me by Micheltorena. This office gave me much

'more power than the one conferred on me by Al-
'varado. Formerly I was obliged to notify the
'government first, and wait for its instructions;
'now I had executive power, could do what I
'thought was proper, and inform the government
'of my acts afterward. To be sure, I never received
'a cent for my duties. The Sacramento and San
'Joaquin valleys I had conquered wholly at my
'own expense. Other officers of the government
'received their pay in cattle and hides from the
'missions, if they were not able to get any cash.
'When Vallejo could get no money from the cus-
'tom house, he would draw an order on his brother,
'who was then governmental administrator at San
'Jose, at that time one of the wealthiest missions.
'Such orders were always honored. Vallejo also
'succeeded in getting possession of almost the en-
'tire property of the missions at San Rafael and
'Solano. For him it was easy enough to become a
'rich man.

'I naturally did not hesitate to give the new
'government the promise which they requested. I
'took the oath of allegiance and received a docu-

[139]

'ment in return, which confirmed me in all my
'property and my titles. *Aguardiente* flowed freely
'and everybody was happy and satisfied.

'Then I began my preparations for the return
'march. Bidwell, who did everything in his power
'to help me, was bold enough to ask the govern-
'ment for the horses which we would need. I had
'lost about a hundred and fifty head in this cam-
'paign. We were told, however, that we could not
'get any horses since they were all scattered over
'the country. Bidwell also tried to get back my
'double rifle, but it could not be found.

'How could I get back without money, without
'provisions, and without horses? Fortunately I met
'a German cooper by the name of Charles Mumm
'for whom I had done many favors in former years.
'Once he had cut staves in the Sacramento Valley,
'which I transported for him to Yerba Buena for
'nothing. This man showed his appreciation by
'bringing me a number of horses, which I paid
'for after my return. Some of my officers and
'men were lucky enough to retain their horses, and

'others had friends from whom they could get
'money or other assistance; so we were ready, after
'many delays, to start upon our return journey.

'When we were ready, Bidwell asked the govern-
'ment to send us back at their own expense and to
'place supplies at our disposal along our route.
'This they refused, of course, but they offered to
'give me credit if I wanted to buy the necessary
'supplies from them; but I knew that this would
'have cost me too much. In addition to Bidwell,
'Doctor Townsend, Juan Vaca, and myself, I had
'to provide for the Indians and the Kanakas, for
'my servants and *vaqueros*. Therefore, I refused
'the offer of the government and decided to live on
'horse flesh if necessary. All I received from the
'government finally was an order to the San Fer-
'nando Mission to supply porridge to my Indians.
'The padre of the mission received me well and
'supplied me with the necessary provisions. I sat
'with the padre alone at his table, while the officers
'sat at a table for themselves. All were provided
'with wine from the cellars of the mission. It was

'on a Sunday and the people from the surround-
'ing districts came to church. After mass there
'was a dance.

'We decided to reach the Fort by way of the
'Tulare Valley. After leaving San Fernando we
'passed through a desert country where we found
'only stunted vegetation and dwarf palm trees.
'Unfortunately we had no guide and the horses
'were on the verge of collapsing from lack of
'water. To escape the desert we struck into the
'mountains and found at last a little stream where
'we pitched our tents.

'Our next stopping place was the San Francis-
'quita farm, situated on the creek of the same
'name. From here I sent out scouts to find a pass
'through the mountains. They found the Tejon
'Pass on a mountain ridge through which the
'Southern Pacific has since built a railroad tunnel.
'What a magnificent view we had from this pass
'and how beautifully green the Tejon Valley
'looked! We marched alternately through snow
'fields and over fine green pasture. It was like de-
'scending the Alps into Italy. Here we rested the

[142]

'whole day in order to give the animals a chance
'to recover.

'The natives whom we met looked sour and were
'not very friendly. We knew that our provisions
'would be scant before we entered the Tulare Val-
'ley. There we would find plenty of horses, which
'were entirely lacking in the Tejon Valley. The
'Indians came to me and asked for permission to
'go ahead alone. They told me that they would
find roots and herbs to live on and that they would
'soon be at home. Since they had no arms, I was
'reluctant to let them go until I was convinced
'that it was the best solution. They actually
'reached the Fort several days ahead of us.

'We white men and one Kanaka continued on
'our slow march, living on the few provisions which
'we had brought from San Fernando and San
'Francisquita. Our greatest difficulty was in cross-
'ing the streams. The King's River, which was
'swollen by the melting snow, was especially diffi-
'cult to cross. We offered the Indians money to
'help us, but they were very saucy and refused.
'By the great Tulare Lake we found another In-

'dian village whose inhabitants likewise refused to
'provide us with anything. We had no fish and no
'meat until we came to a little stream where one
'of my men succeeded in making a fish hook from
'cattle wire and catching a number of fish.

'The horses began to give out again and we
'had to travel very slowly. There were now thir-
'teen men in our party, eight white men, four
'*vaqueros*, and one Kanaka. When we came to the
'Merced River, we had to build a raft in order to
'ferry over. On the other side of the Merced, we
'espied a band of Indian horse thieves, four
'in number, who had with them about twenty
'horses stolen in the San Jose Valley. I told my
'men that we would have to continue our journey
'on foot unless we succeeded in capturing these
'horses. We therefore prepared for an attack,
'charged the horse thieves, drove them off, and
'procured their animals.

'After that we came to the Stanislaus River,
'the worst stream that we had to cross on our
'march. We had to have a raft, but we had no
'hatchets or other tools with which to build one.

'We helped ourselves by lassoing the dry branches
'from trees and made a raft by tying the branches
'together with strings. The Kanaka swam across
'the river with a line which he tied to a tree on the
'opposite shore. Only one man with a little luggage
'could cross the river on the raft at a time; he had
'to lie flat and to ferry himself across by pulling
'the rope. The raft was pulled back by a rope, and
'gradually we all crossed safely. The horses, of
'course, had to swim across, and since the river
'bank was very steep, we had no little difficulty in
'getting them to the shore. The horse thieves had
'in the meantime mobilized their whole village and
'kept on molesting us. We had to keep up a con-
'stant rifle fire while we were building the raft
'and crossing the river.

'On the following night we did not dare to pitch
'camp on account of the hostile Indians. There
'was no path along which we could travel and the
'north star was our only guide. Our provisions
'had long given out and had we not killed an ante-
'lope, we would have been forced to live on horse
'meat entirely. At last we arrived at the Mo-

'kelumne River, where we found horses and pro-
'visions which Major Reading, the commander of
'the Fort in my absence, had sent down for our
'relief. From there we rode home comfortably and
'arrived safely at New Helvetia on April first.

'I embarked on this venture wholly at my own
'expense and I never received any remuneration.
'On the day before the night attack at Buena
'Ventura, I asked Micheltorena to execute the deed
'for the so-called *sobrante* grant in order that my
'family might be guaranteed possession in the
'event that I should be killed. He immediately
'complied with my wish and had one of his two sec-
'retaries make out the deed. He expressed his re-
'gret that he was unable to recompense me for my
'expenses, which by that time amounted to some
'eight thousand dollars, not counting my own serv-
'ices. The secretary who executed the deed was
'Micheltorena's aide-de-camp, Captain Juan Cas-
'tañeda. The document itself I entrusted with
'other papers to the care of John S. Fowler while
'he was acting as my agent. All these records were
'destroyed by fire in 1851; but Castañeda is still

'alive and testified on my behalf several years ago
'before the land commission.

'My object in aiding Micheltorena in this cam-
'paign was to strengthen my position with the
'government and to secure good land titles and
'protection for the immigrants. I had fitted out
'most of the men at my expense and failing in my
'purpose, I lost it all—money, horses, arms, and
'provisions. Fortunately my relations with the new
'government continued to be friendly.'

IX

On the Eve of the Mexican War

THE new Governor, Pio Pico, and his associates continued the feeble attempts of their predecessors to redeem California from its chaotic conditions. During his administration the fate of Upper California as Mexican territory ran its course. After the United States Congress had voted the admission of Texas to the Union in March 1845, a war between the two American republics seemed to have become inevitable. During the summer all California talked about the coming contest, making noisy but ineffective efforts to put the country into some shape for defense. It was apparent that

New Helvetia was destined to play an important rôle in this ensuing struggle—not so much as a bulwark against an invading army from across the Sierras as a rallying point for those foreign elements which were anxious to see the territory a part of the American commonwealth. In the hearts of Vallejo and other patriots the acquisition of Sutter's Fort became a national obligation for which the country should have been willing to make some sacrifices. The easiest way to have secured this strategic location would have been to buy the mortgage from the Russian-American Company and then have forced Sutter to sell his settlement. An agreement to that effect was actually made with the vice-governor of the Company on the twenty-fourth of November, but the matter had not progressed beyond the initial stages when the cannon at the Rio Grande had begun to speak. The alternate project of buying New Helvetia directly and peacefully from the owner likewise came to naught, although Vallejo was strongly in favor of it. There is some evidence that Sutter was not quite so decided in his refusal as he asserted in later years. He certainly would not have played with the idea had the surrender of the Fort to the government spelled real danger to the settlers of the valley. No matter how questionable his business dealings may appear at times—he surely would not have broken faith with his men. But a stipulation, confirming the settlers in their possessions, could have been easily inserted in the bill of sale. The Californians would have fulfilled this obligation. They had meticulously kept their promise given to the adherents of Micheltorena before the surrender in the San Fernando Valley. Moreover, even those foreigners about whose leanings toward the United States there could be no doubt, and who did not enjoy the protection of New Helvetia's guns, were left unmolested.

'After my return I had my hands full setting 'matters right. In the second week of April I was 'obliged to undertake another campaign against 'the natives. The Indians from the vicinity of the 'San Joaquin Mountains had killed Thomas Lind-'say on his farm near the present site of Stockton 'and driven off his cattle. While reconnoitering one

RUINS OF SUTTER'S MILL AT COLOMA

Painting by C. Nahl

HOCK-FARM

FORT SUTTER AFTER ITS RESTORATION

'morning my clerk and loyal companion during
'the recent campaign, Juan Vaca, was shot at my
'side. He was the only man killed in the affray,
'although many were wounded. I was, as usual, the
'first to charge, and a number of arrows pierced
'my clothing. Yet I escaped without injury.

'On the twenty-first of October I received from
'Governor Pico and General Castro a *bandas* or
'proclamation on account of the threatening war
'between the United States and Mexico. At the
'same time orders arrived to stop the immigration
'from the United States, which was greater this fall
'than ever before. I called a meeting of the settlers
'and immigrants for the twenty-third at the Fort,
'where the proclamation was read and discussed.
'Fortunately the government took no steps to
'make me enforce the order.

'A few weeks later, on the eleventh of November,
'1845, a deputation from the government arrived
'at New Helvetia to make an offer for the purchase
'of my establishment. My Indians informed me
'that a number of Spaniards were on the other side
'of the river. I sent Bidwell to see who they were

'and what they wanted. The visitors turned out to
'be General José Castro, Colonel Prudon, Jacob
'Leese, and Andres Castillero, *comisionado* from
'Mexico, whom I had been expecting for several
'days. They came with an escort of about fifteen
'mounted soldiers by way of Sonoma, where Leese
'had joined them. Castillero had been sent by
'President José Herrera to regulate affairs in gen-
'eral, and to make peace with the new government.
'At the same time he was commissioned to effect
'the purchase of my Fort in order to garrison
'it and to put a stop to the flow of immigration.
'They had said all the time that I was holding the
'key to California and could regulate immigration
'to suit myself. This was true, because most of the
'immigrants entered California over the passes
'east of Fort Sutter or through the valley via
'Oregon. I used to make out passports at my
'pleasure, and every official, both in California and
'in Mexico, was obliged to recognize these pass-
'ports. My visitors apologized to Bidwell for not
'having announced their coming in writing, pre-
'tending that it was nothing but simple careless-

'ness. Bidwell reported to me by sending a *vaquero*
'with a note and I gave orders to have the gentle-
'men ferried across the river and brought to the
'Fort. The landing place was at the same spot
'where the *embarcadero* of the city of Sacramento
'is now situated. When the Mexicans had crossed
'the river and approached the Fort, I hoisted the
'Mexican flag and ordered a salute of seven guns.

'I received the distinguished visitors outside the
'gates of my Fort and invited them to enter. The
'officers were quartered in the main building and
'the soldiers in the houses outside of the walls.
'They entered at once upon the purpose of their
'coming; they told me that the government wished
'to buy my Fort with all its improvements and that
'they were authorized to pay one hundred thou-
'sand dollars for it. I was greatly surprised, for
'the idea of selling and moving had never entered
'my mind. All I could tell them, therefore, was that
'I would give the matter careful consideration.
'Thereupon I withdrew to my office in the same
'building and held a consultation with Bidwell,
'Reading, and Locker. I told them what I had been

[153]

'offered for the establishment, and they all thought
'that it was a very large sum. After they had dis-
'cussed the matter for some time, their thoughts
'turned naturally upon their own interests. "What
'shall we do?" they said. "And what will all the
'settlers in the valley do if you abandon us to the
'Mexicans?" This brought about my decision. I
'felt that I was in duty bound to continue my pro-
'tection of the immigrants. Had it not been for this
'consideration, I should have accepted the Mexican
'offer. Often I have regretted not having sold New
'Helvetia at that time, because for this great sacri-
'fice I have been rewarded with nothing but
'ingratitude.

'Castro and Castillero, after having become con-
'vinced that all their efforts had been in vain,
'started on their return trip to Monterey the next
'morning. As they left, the guns of the Fort fired
'another salute. Attended by Bidwell and two or
'three *vaqueros*, I accompanied the officials for
'about twenty miles, as far as the Cosumnes River.
'We had hardly proceeded a mile from the Fort
'when we saw galloping toward us a troop of

'horsemen, about fifty mechanics, *vaqueros*, and
'others under the command of one of my assistants.
' "What is all this?" asked Castro. "Only some of
'my men," I replied, "who would have followed
'us sooner as an escort in your honor, had they
'been able to get their horses together in time."
'As a matter of fact, I said this only because I
'myself was at a loss to understand this cavalcade.
'I was told later that my men had become alarmed
'when they saw me riding away with my enemies.
'They had feared that the Mexicans would kidnap
'me in order to be able to take possession of the
'Fort at their own terms. Neither Bidwell nor I
'had had any such apprehensions; we knew these
'people better than the others.

'When we reached the Cosumnes, I bade good-
'bye to my guests and returned home. But to my
'great surprise, Colonel Prudon appeared that
'same evening in my room. "I hope you will con-
'sider our proposal once more," he said. "We are
'willing to raise our offer considerably. I have been
'authorized by General Castro to offer you as a
'purchase price for New Helvetia all the lands and

'the cattle belonging to the Mission San Jose in
'addition to the sum of one hundred thousand
'dollars." Prudon had been sent, not only because
'he was a very capable man, but also because he
'was one of my old friends and supposed to have
'influence with me. He said that I was probably
'afraid that I would have difficulty in getting my
'money but that I should have no fear, although
'the coffers of the Mexican Government were
'empty. I would receive a handsome down payment
'and orders on the custom house for the balance.
'I knew that I did not have to have any fear in
'that respect, and I knew also that they would
'have paid me a larger sum because they were ex-
'tremely anxious to get possession of the Fort. But
'after repeated consultation with my adherents, I
'felt obliged to turn down this new offer.

'About four weeks later Captain Frémont came
'to the Fort the second time but stayed only a
'few days, from December tenth to December thir-
'teenth. Then he started for the South where he
'was to meet Captain T. Walker.

'On Christmas day of the same year the famous

'overland guide, Captain W. L. Hastings, arrived
'with Dr. Robert Semple and ten other men—the
'last of the several parties who reached New Hel-
'vetia this season directly from the United States.
'They had crossed the Sierras just in the nick of
'time, for a few days later a snowstorm set in by
'which they would have been snowbound in the
'mountains. This was the same storm which pre-
'vented the Donner Party, of whom I have spoken
'above, from crossing the mountains. Captain
'Hastings and his party remained with me all win-
'ter; some of the members I employed at New
'Helvetia.

'On January fourteenth, 1846, Captain Leides-
'dorff, vice-consul for the United States at Yerba
'Buena, and Captain Hinkley, captain of the port
'of Yerba Buena, arrived on a friendly visit. Since
'both men were in uniform, I put on my Mexican
'uniform too, and rode with them toward a certain
'spot on the American River which Leidesdorff
'wished to select for a grant. We had proceeded
'only a mile or two from the Fort when we noticed
'a camp. While I was wondering what camp that

[157]

'could be, I saw Kit Carson coming up to me.
' "Where is Captain Frémont?" I asked him. "Over
'there in his tent," was the reply, "he is tired and
'not up yet." I asked Kit Carson to call him out,
'introduced my companions to him, and told him
'that we were on a little expedition up the river. I
'invited him to join us on our return and to dine
'with me at the Fort. Frémont said that he had ar-
'rived at the spot late at night and that he would
'remove his camp to the bank of the river near the
'Fort. This he did while we continued on our jour-
'ney up the American River. On our return I or-
'dered the firing of the salute of seven guns and
'prepared a sumptuous dinner. Frémont returned
'to his camp the same night, and Leidesdorff and
'Hinkley left for Yerba Buena the next morning.

'I had not the slightest idea why Frémont came
'the second time. Afterward I learned that he had
'gone to Monterey to see the American vice-consul,
'Thomas Larkin, but had been driven back by the
'Californians, who were gravely concerned over
'the activities of a United States army officer in
'the country. I myself was ignorant of his purpose.

'War had not yet been declared, and Frémont
'acted strangely toward me, as if he were guilty of
'some crime. Every few days he would move his
'camp further up the valley.

'I had always been friendly to Frémont and had
'assisted him in every way possible. When he was
'at the Fort the first time, Micheltorena had sent
'a military commission, as mentioned previously,
'to inquire what Frémont was doing at New Hel-
'vetia. I had expected the soldiers and had hurried
'Frémont off before they came. When they arrived
'I told them that he had gone already, and simply
'sent a colorless report to the government. It never
'occurred to me that Frémont had come to the
'country to prepare the way for the annexation of
'California to the United States. True, at his first
'visit, before I had come to an understanding with
'Micheltorena, I had told him that I had all kinds
'of trouble with the Californians. Since I was de-
'termined to declare my independence of both
'Mexico and California, as soon as I felt strong
'enough to do so, I had asked him if I could de-
'clare myself a subject of the United States in

'case my plans should be successful. Frémont had 'replied at that time that it could probably be done 'but that it had to be decided by Congress.

'On January nineteenth, 1846, Frémont took 'passage with eight of his men on board my 'schooner for Yerba Buena. Ten days later the 'boat returned with Jacob Snyder and William 'Sublette, who brought the news to the Fort that 'war was said to have been declared between the 'United States and England. Mexican troops were 'daily expected to arrive in California, and a 'rumor gained ground that California would be 'delivered over to the United States, to forestall 'annexation by Great Britain. On the four-'teenth of March, Doctor Marsh sent a messenger 'with the information that Captain Frémont was 'blockaded near Monterey by Castro and his sol-'diers, who refused to allow him to proceed south 'along the coast. The foreign settlers wanted to 'assist Frémont, but he refused their aid. On 'March the twenty-first he returned to the Fort 'and camped on the other side of the American 'fork. He guarded himself carefully against any

'surprise attack by the Californians, and after a
'few days he left for the upper Sacramento and
'for Oregon.

'Frémont's conduct was extremely mysterious.
'Flitting about the country with an armed body
'of men, he was regarded with suspicion by every-
'body. When he was encamped at Lassen's farm,
'he bought stolen horses from the Indians, paying
'five yards of calico or a few beads for each horse.
'While he was still at Lassen's, I wrote a letter to
'him requesting the return of the stolen horses that
'he had bought from the Indians. I was still a
'magistrate and an officer of the Mexican Govern-
'ment at that time, and I deemed it my duty to
'enter this protest. Frémont made no reply to my
'letter and never forgave me for having written it.

'On April twenty-eighth Lieutenant Archibald
'Gillespie, who was then at an Indian village about
'ten miles below the Fort, sent word through an
'Indian messenger that he would visit me after
'sunset. When he arrived, he asked me if I knew
'where Frémont had his camp and told me that he
'had secret dispatches from his government for

[161]

'him. When I told him that Frémont was in
'the northern part of California, he asked me for
'horses and for a guide to overtake him. I allowed
'him to take my favorite mule, for which I had
'paid three hundred dollars. He returned it wind-
'broken, and that was the only profit that I got
'out of this affair. When Gillespie arrived at Las-
'sen's farm, Peter Lassen had told him that Fré-
'mont must be a good distance on his way to
'Oregon. Since the agent of the United States
'Government insisted on finding him, Lassen sup-
'plied him with horses and accompanied him per-
'sonally. They found Frémont at the Ambuscade
'Creek on the ninth of May, involved in a fight
'with Indians. When Frémont read the dispatches
'of the American Government, he returned to Cali-
'fornia immediately. Lieutenant Gillespie returned
'to the Fort on the thirtieth of May and left two
'days later for Yerba Buena on board my
'schooner.

'While the country was in a state of great
'excitement and the opening of hostilities was

'awaited daily, I was obliged to undertake my last
'campaign against the natives. The Mokelumne
'Indians were engaged by Castro to revolutionize
'all the Indians against me, to massacre the farm-
'ers, and to burn their houses and wheat fields.
'These Mokelumne Indians had great possessions
'and many of them were finely dressed and
'equipped with arms. Some of them came on a
'friendly visit to my Fort and had long conversa-
'tions with the influential men among my Indians.
'One night a number of Indians entered my *po-*
'*trero*, a kind of enclosure for animals, and tried
'to drive away the horses. The guard at the Fort
'heard a distant noise and spread an alarm. I left
'immediately with six well-armed men, but the rob-
'bers succeeded in making their escape into the
'woods, where the city of Sacramento now stands.

'On June third I left in company with Major
'Reading and with most of the men in my employ
'in order to put an end to the danger of an Indian
'uprising. When we crossed the Mokelumne River
'on rafts, one of them capsized, whereby we lost

'a number of rifles and pistols, a goodly supply of
'ammunition, and the clothes of about twenty-four
'men. Major Reading and another man just
'escaped being drowned. Some of the men who had
'lost their arms and clothing had to be left behind
'while the rest of us marched on toward the Cala-
'veras River, without, however, finding the enemy.
'At sunrise we took a little rest and dispatched a
'reconnoitering party. Suddenly a dog appeared
'at our camp, which led us to conclude that the
'enemy could not be very far away, and a little
'later a messenger came galloping with the news
'that the advance guard was engaged with the
'enemy. We immediately rushed to the aid of our
'men, some of whom had already been wounded
'and were unable to continue the fight. Upon our
'arrival the enemy retired and fled to a large
'cellar-like hole on the bank of the Calaveras. Pro-
'tected by brush and trees, they continued shoot-
'ing their arrows at us, although we had them
'blockaded and killed a good many of them. When,
'however, our ammunition gave out, we thought it

'prudent to leave the scene slowly, making the In-
'dians believe that we intended to camp. But as
'soon as we were out of their sight, we started on a
'forced march, crossed the Mokelumne and reached
'the Fort on June seventh.'

X

The American Conquest

DURING the summer months of 1846, California's
political future was decided. After General Mariano Paredes and his anti-American Centralists
had succeeded in gaining the upper hand in the
affairs of Mexico, President Polk declared war
upon the southern neighbor on the thirteenth of
May, and the first shots were fired on the Texas
frontier long before the hostilities in California
started. With Frémont's return from Oregon, the
settlers of the Sonoma district started the so-called
Bear Flag revolt, and soon after that Frémont
assumed the rôle of a conqueror in northern Cali-

fornia. At the beginning of July Commodore John D. Sloat's squadron anchored off Monterey, and on the seventh of this month the United States marines took possession of the capital and declared the annexation of the territory. The forces of General Castro dissolved into thin air, and a few local uprisings were speedily suppressed, though not without some shedding of blood. In January of the following year the land was so firmly in the hands of the United States that General Stephen W. Kearny, who had arrived from Santa Fe with a squadron of cavalry, and Commodore Robert Stockton, the successor to Sloat, could indulge in a somewhat undignified controversy as to who had the right to rule the territory. During this controversy the California career of Frémont came to an ignominious end. General Kearny had to make full use of his authority as a superior officer to force Frémont to give up the governorship to which he had been appointed by Stockton. He left the state as a virtual prisoner and was subsequently courtmartialed.

The part which Sutter was destined to play

during the war was hardly more enviable than that of Frémont. There can be no doubt that his sympathies were on the side of the United States, if for no other reason than for the fact that there could be no question about the outcome of the struggle. But being a high Mexican official and on friendly terms with the government, he would have acted dishonorably, had he assumed the part for which he had really been slated by the circumstances, namely to assume the leadership in the revolt of the settlers. So he took the only sensible attitude by remaining passive, bending to the *force majeur* when the filibusters knocked at the gate of his Fort and when he was ordered to hoist the Stars and Stripes. In August he took the oath of allegiance to the United States but was given the rank of a mere lieutenant of the United States army with a monthly salary of fifty dollars. In his reminiscences, he attempts in vain to ascribe to himself a more important character than he actually played during the Mexican War. Yet, his activities before the American conquest fully justify General Sherman's flattering remarks, which were incorporated in the resolution of the *Associated Pioneers of Territorial Days in California* at the occasion of Sutter's demise: "To General Sutter more than to any other actor in the events which made California a part of our national domain, is due the permanent acquisition of that rich and beautiful region of our country."

'A few weeks after our return Commodore Sloat 'arrived at Monterey and took formal possession 'of the country. Mexico owed a large sum of money 'to England, and the British had hoped that they 'would receive California in payment of the Mexi-'can debt. In my opinion, California would doubt-'less be English today if Sloat had arrived a day 'later. Francisco Arce, a lieutenant in the Cali-'fornia army, said to me one day: "California is 'like a pretty girl, everybody wants her." Imme-'diately after Sloat had occupied Monterey, a 'United States man-of-war, the *Portsmouth*, Cap-'tain John B. Montgomery, took possession of the 'harbor of Yerba Buena. In Sonoma and New

'Helvetia the war had started several weeks before
'the forces of the United States occupied the prin-
'cipal ports.

'Frémont returned from the north during the
'latter part of May, and camped at the Buttes
'near New Mecklenburg. He gathered around
'him all the discontented settlers, and moved his
'force gradually down the valley. On the evening
'of June eighth Lieutenant Arce arrived with eight
'men at the Fort, driving a large flock of horses
'from Sonoma, which General Vallejo was sending
'for the California cavalry at Monterey. He was
'obliged to come by way of New Helvetia because
'he had to use my ferry to cross the river. The
'party left early the next day and reached Mur-
'phy's place. On June tenth five or six armed men
'under the command of Ezekiel Meritt arrived at
'the Fort in pursuit of Arce. Meritt was an old
'mountaineer, who had been in my employ for a
'long time, but now he was recruiting for Frémont.
'He told me that he was going to overtake Arce
'and seize the horses for Frémont. Arce's men were
'afraid to fight and Meritt could confiscate the

'horses without any serious resistance. Meritt al-
'lowed each Californian one horse in order to be
'able to get to Monterey.

'During the next few days Frémont made his
'appearance before the gates of my Fort with
'his entire force. Meritt, Carson, and a great many
'settlers, in all about a hundred men, were with
'him. I opened the gates of the Fort and the sol-
'diers came and went at their pleasure. Frémont
'regarded me as his ally. By the simple act of
'throwing open my gates I had indeed renounced
'my allegiance to the Mexican Government and
'had thrown my lot with the forces of the United
'States. Frémont, like everybody else, knew I was
'loyal to the cause; however, although we had no
'bad words, he appeared shy of me. When I told
'Kit Carson that Frémont seemed to be unfriendly
'toward me, he replied: "Remember that letter."

'Frémont returned to his camp a mile or two up
'the American River and left at my Fort a small
'garrison of eight or ten men under the command
'of Lieutenant Edward Kern. I believed at first
'that these men were to assist me, but I discovered

'soon that they were left to act as spies over me.
'Frémont, taking with him all of my workmen and
'all of my best Indians, set out for Sonoma. I
'remained in absolute command of the Fort; no
'attempt was made to supersede me. As a matter
'of fact, I was generally regarded as an officer of
'the United States Government.

'On June thirteenth a launch of the American
'man-of-war *Portsmouth* came up the river to the
'Fort. The launch was under the command of Lieu-
'tenant Hunter, who was accompanied by
'Lieutenant Gillespie, Purser Watmough, and
'Doctor Duvall. A few days later, on June six-
'teenth, Meritt and Kit Carson reached the Fort
'with the news that Sonoma was in the hands of
'the Americans. The same evening there arrived
'at my Fort General Vallejo, Lieutenant-Colonel
'Prudon, Jacob Leese, Salvador Vallejo, and Julio
'Carrillo, a nephew of General Vallejo. They were
'guarded by fifteen or twenty of Frémont's men
'and were entrusted in my care as prisoners of war.
'They had been arrested that same morning while
'they were still lying in bed. Immediately after

[172]

'Vallejo's arrest, the Bear Flag was raised at So-
'noma by a band of robbers under Frémont's
'command.

'When the prisoners arrived at the Fort, I
'placed my best rooms at their disposal and treated
'them with every consideration. I did not approve
'of this arrest at all; I believed it to be wrong and
'unnecessary. The gentlemen took their meals at
'my table and walked with me in the evening.
'Neither did I place a guard before the door of the
'room, nor did I order any soldiers to accompany
'us when we were walking. I thought that it was
'wholly unnecessary to be more severe with them.
'They were men of property and there was no
'danger of their attempting to escape.

'Four or five days later Frémont, who became
'stronger every day, appeared again with a strong
'force at my Fort and complained that I treated
'his prisoners too kindly. His men had told him
'that my prisoners ate at my table and that I
'walked with them, and Frémont asked me harshly:
' "Don't you know how to treat prisoners of war?"

' "Indeed I do, Captain Frémont," I replied. "I

'have been a prisoner myself. Take charge of these
'men yourself; I don't want to have anything fur-
'ther to do with them."

'Fremont then asked me into whose charge he
'could possibly give them and inquired about the
'trustworthiness of my clerk. I told him that Mr.
'Locker was a gentleman and absolutely depend-
'able.

'Locker, however, did not like his job as guard
'either, and he left a short while later to join the
'volunteers. The prisoners were then placed in
'charge of Bidwell, who allowed them just as much
'liberty as they enjoyed when they were in my
'care. He taught Prudon English and received in-
'struction in Spanish in return. I visited the pris-
'oners frequently and often sat and talked with
'them until one day Doctor Townsend warned me
'not to be too friendly with them if I did not wish
'to become a prisoner in my own house. I followed
'his well meant advice and did not visit them again
'until we were under the American flag.

'Frémont, who had been strengthened in the
'meantime by Major Reading and my trappers,

'a party of men who came down from Oregon, and
'two cannon from the Fort, left then for the south
'to join Commodore Stockton. He had no reason to
'be proud of his forces; some of his officers could
'not even write their names. Bidwell, who served as
'a lieutenant under Frémont, was ashamed of such
'conditions. He was given charge of the Mission
'of San Luis Rey, which he administered so well
'that the Indians came back and went to work.
'Unfortunately he did not remain long in charge
'of it. Frémont himself was engaged in the lower
'country where he was made governor by Stockton.
'When General Kearny arrived and put an end to
'Frémont's autocratic dealings, the latter made
'himself so obnoxious that the General was obliged
'to make him prisoner.

'Meanwhile Lieutenant Joseph Warren Revere
'with a detachment of sailors from the *Portsmouth*
'had taken command of Sonoma under orders from
'Captain Montgomery. The Bear Flag was hauled
'down and the Stars and Stripes hoisted in its
'stead. On the evening of the tenth of July Lieu-
'tenant Revere sent William Scott with an Ameri-

[175]

'can flag and the order to hoist it at sunrise. A
'long time before daybreak I had the whole Fort
'alarmed and my guns ready. When the Star-
'Spangled Banner slowly rose on the flag staff,
'the cannon began to fire and continued until
'nearly all the windows were broken. Some of the
'people around the Fort made long faces, because
'they thought that they would have had a better
'chance to rob and to plunder if we had remained
'under the Bear Flag. The Sonoma prisoners, not
'knowing what was going on, were greatly sur-
'prised. I went to them and said: "Now, gentlemen,
'we are under the protection of this great flag, and
'we shall henceforth not be afraid to talk to one
'another. Frémont has acted like a tyrant." They
'all rejoiced that the anarchy was over. However,
'it was not until a few weeks later that Commo-
'dore Stockton sent orders to release the prisoners.
'They thanked me for the many kindnesses which
'I had shown them, and General Vallejo and I, who
'had been at odds for a long time, became good
'friends henceforth.

'In the meantime Captain Montgomery had

'organized garrisons at Sonoma, Yerba Buena,
'San Jose, and other places. Lieutenant John S.
'Misroon came to drill the forces at Fort Sutter.
'The garrison consisted then of about a hundred
'men, half white and half Indians, many of them
'my former soldiers. I retained my command of the
'Fort until the arrival of the New York Volunteers.

'Before the coming of General Kearny the
'Californians made serious attempts to drive
'the Americans out of the country; Frémont
'had the greatest difficulties to maintain himself
'and urgently solicited my aid. He wanted me to
'come down to his headquarters, and when I sent
'word that I was unable to do so, Colonel William
'H. Russell, whom he called his secretary of state,
'came to the Fort. Frémont had told him that I
'was the only man who could control the Indians.
'I informed Colonel Russell that Commodore
'Montgomery had ordered me to garrison and hold
'the Fort. I considered it my duty to stay at New
'Helvetia but told him that I would send Frémont
'all the help I could. Just at that time there hap-
'pened to be encamped by the Feather River a

'large company of Walla Walla Indians led by
'their chief, Yellow Serpent. They came down from
'Oregon to hunt and trade in the valley, and to
'seek justice for the murder of a young chief, the
'son of Yellow Serpent, who had been killed some
'time before during a quarrel with one of my men.
'Their appearance at the northern frontier caused
'some of the settlers to flee post haste to my Fort,
'and the exaggerated reports caused such a panic
'throughout California that a massacre of the
'Walla Wallas was just barely avoided. I knew
'that they were good fighters; so I asked them if
'they would go to Frémont's assistance and told
'them that they would be paid for their services.
'Being a war-like people, many of them were glad
'to go. François Gendreau, a Canadian who had
'a Walla Walla woman for a wife, I made captain
'of the detachment. From among the natives on
'the Stanislaus and Mokelumne, old horse thieves
'who had reformed, I formed another company and
'placed it in charge of José Jesus, a christianized
'Indian. In addition to these, I dispatched about
'twenty white men. An American by the name of

'Charles Burroughs I made commander of the
'whole force. Unfortunately, he was killed in the
'first encounter with the enemy at Natividad, on
'November the sixteenth. The Walla Wallas
'brought back many trophies and spoils; a num-
'ber of them were clad in the uniforms taken from
'the Mexicans whom they had killed. They them-
'selves lost in the whole campaign only one man.
'When they returned to New Helvetia, they had
'not yet received their pay and, believing that I
'had deceived them, threatened to declare war upon
'me. I pacified them by giving them a lot of old,
'broken-down government horses, stamped U. S.,
'which were roaming about the Fort. On their re-
'turn march to Oregon, they behaved very badly
'and did a lot of damage. They caught and mal-
'treated a number of Indians from California
'tribes and stole horses from me and the other
'settlers.

'On May twenty-fourth, 1847, a detachment of
'Stevenson's regiment of the New York Volunteers
'arrived at the Fort to relieve my Indian soldiers.
'The commander of the detachment was Lieuten-

'ant Anderson, to whom I turned over the com-
'mand of the Fort. The detachment consisted of
'one-half of Company C, which was quartered at
'New Helvetia, while the other half of the company
'was stationed at Sonoma. The officers of the de-
'tachment ate at my table, while the enlisted men
'cooked their own rations. The New York Volun-
'teers remained at the Fort for several months.
'After the discovery of gold most of them deserted
'and went off to the mines. The regiment was dis-
'banded soon afterwards.

'For all my services during the Mexican war I
'did not receive a single cent. Neither were my sol-
'diers ever paid. The muster rolls of the Indians
'were lost and they complained that the Americans
'did not pay their soldiers any better than the
'Mexicans.

'On June thirteenth, 1847, General Kearny,
'his staff, and a few other gentlemen passed the
'Fort on their return march to the East. A salute
'was fired and the garrison was lined up on parade.
'The next day I gave a dinner in honor of the
'United States general. Three days later the of-

'ficers and their escort departed for the mountains. 'Frémont left the country in the retinue of the 'general, more or less as a prisoner. On the seven- 'teenth of the following month, Commodore Stock- 'ton and a strong detachment of American sol- 'diers arrived in the valley, likewise on their re- 'turn across the mountains. I visited him at his 'camp on Bear Creek and presented him with my 'best horse.

'An unfortunate accident occurred on August 'fourth. Major J. H. Cloud, the paymaster, and 'Captain Joseph Folsom, the quartermaster of the 'United States forces, had come to the Fort to pay 'off the garrison. Major Cloud had bought a pair 'of large Spanish spurs from one of the men. I ac- 'companied the two officers on horseback, and 'about half a mile from the Fort, Major Cloud was 'thrown from his horse, which was not accustomed 'to the Spanish spurs. The doctor of the garrison 'and my own physician tried in vain to save his 'life; he died the same evening without having re- 'gained consciousness. He was buried with military 'honors two days later.

'On August twenty-fifth, finally, the Mormon
'battalion under Captain Jefferson Hunt passed
'New Helvetia on its way to the Great Salt Lake.
'They bought provisions and had blacksmith work
'done, and I delivered to them the government
'horses for which they had orders. About eighty of
'the discharged Mormons I took into my employ,
'giving them work as mechanics or as laborers.

'The Mormon battalion had come into the
'country shortly after the arrival of General
'Kearny. It consisted of about eight hundred or a
'thousand men, all of them, officers and men, being
'Mormons, except its commander, Philip St.
'George Cook, who was a captain in the regular
'army and subsequently a general. They all came
'from the Missouri River, and it was my impres-
'sion that they had been organized at Council
'Bluffs. When they arrived in California to partic-
'ipate in the war, the armed conflict was practi-
'cally over and they were disbanded and paid off.
'Since they intended to settle in Utah, they were
'allowed to retain their arms. A great number,
'however, remained in the country temporarily.

'Jared Sheldon employed about twenty men to
'build a grist mill on the Cosumnes River. Others
'found work in San Jose, and I hired about eighty
'of them as mentioned above. They were very glad
'to earn some money in order to buy horses and cat-
'tle for their new homes at the Salt Lake to which
'they all longed to go. They were very good people
'and in settling accounts I never had any difficulty
'with them.'

XI

The Discovery of Gold

THE year following the American conquest was
the most prosperous and promising in the history
of New Helvetia. Within the short space of eight
years, the activities of the enterprising Swiss had
changed the wilderness into bustling communities.
In December of 1847, Sutter, since April United
States sub-Indian agent for his district, could report that the population of the Sacramento Valley
numbered 289 white people and 479 tame Indians,
besides over 21,000 wild Indians. Sixty houses had
been erected in the territory of which Fort Sutter
formed the nucleus. A tannery, six mills, and a

number of industries were operated by Sutter and his neighbors. Over 14,000 *fanegas* of wheat were harvested during the season, and the live stock was counted by the thousands. Three miles below the Fort the town of Sutterville was laid out and gave promise of a healthy development. A few good harvests would have sufficed to rid New Helvetia of its debts, and Sutter could hope to become in due time the richest man of the Pacific Coast.

'After the war things prospered for me. I found 'a good market for my products among the new-'comers and the people in the Bay district. My 'manufactures increased and there was no lack of 'skilled mechanics. I had a number of looms, and 'the natives were taught to weave blankets and to 'make hats. People came to buy leather, shoes, 'saddles, hats, spurs, bridles, and other articles 'which were turned out by my shops. Agriculture 'increased until I had several hundred men work-'ing in the harvest fields, and to feed them I had to 'kill four or sometimes five oxen daily. I could raise '40,000 bushels of wheat without trouble, reap the 'crop with sickles, thrash it with hones, and winnow

'it in the wind. There were thirty plows running
'with fresh oxen every morning. The Russians
'were the chief customers for my agricultural
'products. I had at the time twelve thousand head
'of cattle, two thousand horses and mules, between
'ten and fifteen thousand sheep, and a thousand
'hogs. My best days were just before the discovery
'of gold.

'The mill at the Fort had for a long time been
'inadequate for the output of flour, and I felt
'keenly the necessity of a mill with a larger ca-
'pacity. I therefore decided to erect a large grist
'mill at Brighton on the American River. On the
'twenty-eighth of May, 1847, two millwrights,
'Marshall and Gingery, commenced to work on the
'mill race. The site was about four miles above the
'Fort where we could get a good fall of water by
'building a dam and digging a race about four
'miles long. The mill was not yet completed when
'gold was discovered. A large building had been
'erected, the necessary wheels and four pairs of
'mill stones were ready to be installed. Everything
'would have been in working order if the discovery

'of gold had been kept secret six weeks longer.

'A more difficult problem was the erection of a
'sawmill. There was no timber in the valley and it
'was necessary to go into the intermediary moun-
'tains to find a suitable place for this mill.

'Now there was in my employ the above-men-
'tioned John Marshall, a man of Scotch extraction
'and a native of New Jersey. He had been with me
'since the war and I esteemed him highly as a good
'mechanic. He made plows, looms, spinning wheels,
'and similar things. He was a spiritualist and a
'very queer person. I always considered him half
'crazy although I could get along with him very
'well. With everybody else, to be sure, he was in-
'volved in continual quarrels. He used to dress in
'buckskin and wear a *serape.*

'With this man I discussed the possibility of
'building a sawmill in the mountains. He believed
'that he could do it, and I was sure that I could
'not find a more dependable man for the job. I
'agreed to pay all the expenses and to give him
'an interest in the mill. In view of its remoteness
'and the large number of men necessary for its con-

'struction, the saw mill meant a heavy financial 'burden from the very beginning.

'On the twenty-first of July Marshall left for 'the mountains with an Indian chief, Nerio, in 'search of a site for the mill. We decided to build 'it at Cul-luma or Coloma, on the south fork of the 'American River. Since all the provisions and ma-'chinery had to be brought up from the Fort, I 'had the Indians build a wagon road to Coloma. 'On August twenty-eighth Marshall and John 'Wimmer left for the mill site, followed soon by the 'Wimmer family, seventeen Mormons, and five 'other men. Mrs. Wimmer was the only woman in 'the party and was to cook for the workers.'

Five months later when the sawmill was almost completed, the first particles of gold were picked up in the tail race by Marshall. The diary of Henry Bigler, one of the Mormons, fixes the date of the fateful event as the twenty-fourth of January, 1848.

The discovery was no great surprise to the people of California. Visiting naturalists had repeatedly called attention to the existence of alluvial gold deposits along the rivers flowing from the Sierras, and rumors of finds were numerous during the years before the discovery. In the Santa Feliciana Cañon near Los Angeles gold had actually been found, and a placer had been worked since 1842 with moderate success. Baptiste Ruelle, an old Canadian trapper, who had been one of the prospectors at this place and later had entered Sutter's employment, claimed in 1843 to have discovered gold on the American River. He showed Sutter and Bidwell a few grains of the precious metal and requested two Indians, two mules and the necessary outfit to follow up his discovery. But Sutter and his clerk, not believing the story, refused. In the following year Pablo Gutierrez, a farm hand at the Hock-Farm, confided to Bidwell that he had discovered gold on the Bear Creek, and the two intended to go for a search when the revolution of 1845 interrupted their plans. Pablo was hanged as a spy during the campaign, and Bidwell's later single-handed efforts proved to be fruitless.

So it was left to the Scotch-American carpenter

to have his name immortalized as the discoverer of gold in California.

'One rainy evening in January 1848, Marshall, 'dripping with water, hurried excitedly into my 'office next to the guard house. He asked to see me 'alone in the "big house" where my private office 'and the clerk's office were located. I was utterly 'surprised, because the day before I had sent up 'everything he required, mill iron and provisions. 'I could not imagine what he wanted, yet I con-'ducted him to my private rooms, which were fur-'nished with old, clumsy laurel wood furniture 'made by the Russians at Fort Ross. We entered 'and I shut the door behind me. Marshall asked me 'if the door was locked. "No," I replied, "but I 'shall gladly lock it." I knew that he was a very 'strange man, and I took the whole thing as a 'whim of his. There was no gun in the room, but I 'was not in the least afraid of him. I supposed he 'acted so queerly because he wanted to tell me some 'secret which he considered important.

'He first said to me: "Are we alone?"

'When I replied in the affirmative, he said: "I 'want two bowls of water."

'I rang the bell for a servant and the bowls of 'water were brought in.

' "Now I want a stick of red wood," said Mar-'shall, "and some twine and some sheets of copper."

' "But, Marshall," I replied, "why do you need 'all these things?"

' "I want to make some scales," he answered.

' "Well," I said, "I have enough scales in the 'apothecary shop."

' "Oh," said Marshall, "I did not think of that." 'I went myself and got some scales.

'When I returned with them, I shut the door but 'did not lock it again. I considered that entirely 'unnecessary because the door led to my bedroom. 'Now Marshall pulled out of his trousers pocket a 'white cotton rag which contained something rolled 'up in it. Just as he was unfolding it to show me 'the contents, the door opened and the clerk, who 'knew nothing of our presence, passed through the 'room.

' "There," exclaimed Marshall, quickly thrust-
'ing the cotton cloth back into his pocket, "didn't
'I tell you that we had listeners?"

'I appeased him, ordered the clerk to retire, and
'locked the door. Then he brought out his mysteri-
'ous secret again. Opening the cloth, he held it be-
'fore me in his hand. It contained what might have
'been about an ounce and a half of gold dust in
'flakes and grains. The largest piece was not quite
'as large as a pea, and the smallest was hardly the
'size of a pin head.

' "I believe this is gold," said Marshall, "but the
'people at the mill laughed at me and called me
'crazy."

'I carefully examined it and said to him: "Well,
'it looks like gold. Let us test it."

'Then I went to the apothecary shop, got *aqua
'fortis* and applied it. The stuff stood the test.

'Marshall asked me if I had any silver. I said I
'had and produced a few dollar pieces. Then we
'placed an equal quantity in weight of gold in one
'scale and silver in the other. Dropping the two in
'the bowls of water, the gold went down and out-

'weighed the silver under water. Finally, I brought
'out a volume of the Encyclopedia Americana,
'a copy of which happened to be on my book
'shelf, to see what other tests could be applied.
'Then I said to him: "I believe this is the finest
'kind of gold."

'Marshall insisted that I accompany him to the
'mill. It was about supper time and the rain con-
'tinued unabated. So I said to him: "You had bet-
'ter eat supper now. Early tomorrow morning, as
'soon as I have given my orders and arranged the
'affairs of the day, I shall go up with you." But
'Marshall would not wait for supper or for any-
'thing else. He mounted his horse and rode off into
'the rainy night.

'The discovery of gold was not entirely unex-
'pected. As early as 1841, James Dana, the min-
'eralogist of the scientific staff of Commodore
'Wilkes' exploring squadron, told me that he had
'found the strongest proof of the existence of gold
'in the vicinity of Mount Shasta and further south.
'A short time afterwards the Swedish scientist
'Doctor G. M. W. Sandels visited me. As time did

[193]

'not permit him to stay very long, he only explored
'a part of the country in a great hurry. But he
'told me also that he had found sure signs of gold
'and was very sorry that he could not explore the
'Sierra Nevada. He did not encourage me to open
'and work mines because it was uncertain whether
'it would pay; it would probably be profitable
'only for a government. So I thought it more pru-
'dent to stick to the plow although I knew that the
'country was rich in gold and other minerals. An
'old attached Mexican servant, Pablo Gutierrez,
'who had followed me to California from the
'United States as soon as he had learned that I was
'here, and who understood a great deal about
'working in the placers, was the next to tell me that
'there were certain signs of gold in the mountains
'on Bear Creek. He told me that he would go to
'work right after his return from the campaign of
'1845. Unfortunately, he became a victim of his
'patriotism. Strange it was, to be sure, that the
'Indians had never brought a piece of gold to me,
'although they very often delivered other things
'which they found in the ravines. I always re-

'quested them to bring curiosities from the moun-
'tains to the Fort and I recompensed them for
'their efforts. I received all kinds of animals, birds,
'plants, young trees, wild fruit, pipe clay, stones,
'red ochre, etc., but never a particle of gold.

'During the night the thought burst upon my
'mind that a curse might rest upon this discovery.
'Of course, I knew nothing of the extent of the vein
'discovered, but whether it amounted to much or
'to little—I was convinced that it would greatly in-
'terfere with my plans. From the very beginning I
'knew what the outcome would be, and it was a very
'melancholy ride on which I started the next morn-
'ing.

'Attended by my sergeant and one of my sol-
'diers, both Indians, I left early for Coloma. When
'we had traveled about half of the way, I saw
'ahead of me something moving in the bushes by
'the road.

'Turning to my attendant I asked: "What can
'that be?"

'He replied: 'It is the same man who was with
you last night."

'When we rode up to the place, sure enough, it 'was Marshall. It was still raining very hard, and 'I asked him: "Have you been here all night?"

' "No," was the reply, "I spent the night at the 'mill and came back this far to meet you."

'During our ride to the mill Marshall was still 'very restless. He believed that the whole country 'around was rich with gold. When we arrived he 'went with me to the mill race. Laborers were at 'work widening and deepening the race. He told 'them to quit work and to let the water run 'through. After the water had washed the gravel 'and the dirt away, Marshall ordered the water to 'be stopped again, and we went hunting for little 'pieces of metal such as Marshall had brought 'down. I picked up some gold, and Marshall and 'the Mormons gave me what they had found. Then 'I said: "I shall have a finger ring made of this 'gold as soon as I can get hold of a goldsmith." 'This ring weighs about an ounce and a half and 'bears my coat of arms and the inscription: "The 'first gold discovered in January 1848." '

Sutter has given a fairly accurate account of

these eventful days, except that he has condensed the happenings of several days into the short space of twenty-four hours. The terse entries of the *New Helvetia Diary* tell the story as follows:

Wednesday, January twenty-sixth: "Dispatched a wagon with six hogs to the sawmill in the mountains. John Wimmer left."

Friday, January twenty-eighth: "Mr. Marshall arrived from the mountains on very important business."

Saturday, January twenty-ninth: "Marshall left for the mountains."

Tuesday, February first: "Left in the evening for the sawmill in the mountains and camped on the dam."

February second to fifth: "Absent."

Wednesday, February ninth: "Dispatched two wagons to the sawmill in the mountains with Jacob Wittmer."

Monday, February fourteenth: "Wittmer returned with the two wagons from the mountains and told everybody of the gold mines there, and brought a few samples with him."

Sutter's Own Story

Sutter's account of gathering the "first gold found in California" loses its dramatic effect for those who know that the Captain was the victim of a practical joke. The workers of the mill, anxious to have the "old cap" let his well-filled bottle make the round, salted the tail race liberally with gold in order to put him in a good mood. The punch was unfortunately taken out of the joke by one of the Wimmer boys who happened to pass the place shortly before Sutter's arrival and was not slow in picking up as much as he could. However, enough of the precious metal seemed to have been left to provide the material for the famous ring, and the workers were doubtless rewarded for the effort by a "civilized drink" from New Helvetia's distillery.

'I gathered all the working men around and 'told them that the yellow metal was doubtless 'gold. I asked them to keep the discovery secret for 'six weeks so that my flour mill could be finished. 'They were all willing to fulfill my wish.

'But this was not to be. Women and whiskey let 'the secret out.

'I remained in Coloma several days and returned

'to the Fort on the fifth of February. Since the
'men at the mill were in need of provisions, I sent
'one of my teamsters, a Swiss by the name of Jacob
'Wittmer, to Coloma. I should have done wiser to
'send one of my Indians. After the teamster had
'delivered the goods, he strolled about the mill and
'met Mrs. Wimmer's children. "We have gold,"
'they cried. When the man laughed at them, the
'mother of the children became angry and ex-
'claimed: "Well, you need not laugh. It is true, we
'have found gold. Look here, what do you call
'that?" She little knew what consequences this
'thoughtless wagging of her tongue would have.

'Wittmer picked some gold and returned to the
'Fort. At that time Samuel Brannan and George
'Smith, a relative of the great Mormon prophet,
'now high in the Church of Utah, kept a store in
'one of my outhouses near the Fort. Aside from
'my own, this was the first store opened in the
'Sacramento Valley. There were a good many set-
'tlers who brought hides, tallow, and skins to this
'Mormon store and received manufactured articles
'in return. George McKinstry, who was with me at

'that time, called it the "shirt-tail store," for every
'time I wanted a few things for my Indians, the
'proprietors exclaimed: "Oh, you will break the
'assortment!" Nevertheless, this store assumed
'great importance after the discovery of gold.

'Now it was a fundamental and unalterable
'principle of the "shirt-tail store" that whiskey
'would not be sold on credit. This was altogether
'too choice an article to be sold on time. The Swiss
'teamster was ordinarily dry, but on this day he
'wanted to have a bottle of brandy to celebrate the
'event. He presented himself at the counter, where
'he formerly had been refused alcohol without cash,
'and called for his poison, at the same time proudly
'producing his gold dust.

' "What is that? You know very well that liquor
'means cash money," exclaimed Brother Smith
'angrily.

' "This is money," replied the teamster, "it is
'gold."

' "Damn you, do you mean to insult me?" roared
'Smith.

' "Go to the Fort and ask the Captain if you 'don't believe me."

'Smith came to the Fort in hot haste and said: ' "Your man came to me and said that this is gold. 'Of course, I know that he is lying and I told him 'so."

' "Nevertheless, it is gold," said I. What else 'could I do? The secret was out.

'Smith sent a note to Brannan, who immediately 'came up with a whole crowd at his heels.

'Now that God had given gold to the Church, 'the Church must build a temple. Brannan rallied 'the hosts of heaven and levied an assessment of 'thirty per cent, afterwards reduced to ten per 'cent, on their increased profits. With this money a 'temple to the Lord was to be built. Brannan built 'several houses, but to this day I don't know of any 'Mormon temple in California. He was to supply 'goods to the Mormons, and the gold which these 'people were to dig was to be divided among Bran-'nan, the diggers, and the Lord. But Brannan, who 'held the keys to the whiskey locker, received the

'largest share. In other words, Brannan's store be-
'came an institution and its owner waxed rich.
'When Brigham Young sent a messenger from
'the Salt Lake to get the Church's share of the
'Lord's tithes, Brannan retorted: "You go back
'and tell Brigham Young that I'll give up the
'Lord's money when he sends me a receipt signed
'by the Lord, and no sooner." '

XII

The Argonaut Invasion

INCREDIBLE as it may be, the momentous event of the discovery of gold, which was to have the most far-reaching consequences in the affairs of the world, caused at first little or no excitement in California. And this in spite of the fact that women and whiskey were by no means the only agents by which the secret leaked out within a few weeks. The laborers at the mill continued work as if nothing had happened, except that they spent their Sundays prospecting for gold instead of shooting deer or picking flowers. The mill was finished on the eleventh of March and started to turn out the much needed lumber. Some Mormons went prospecting to the American River to while away their time until the march to the Great Salt Lake, scheduled for the first of June, and the *New Helvetia Diary* records that a few curious people went up to the mines only to return a few days later.

Sutter himself went about quietly and consistently to secure the fruits of the sudden discovery. He assembled the chiefs of the Indian tribes living around the mill site, and in payment of some goods obtained a three years' lease of some ten square miles around Coloma. His application for preëmption to the tract, to be sure, was denied by the military governor, Richard Mason. The intelligence that the treaty of peace had been signed a few weeks before had as yet not reached California, and the laws of the United States could not be applied in a country which was still held by right of conquest only. The attempt to have the lease of the Coloma Valley confirmed had, however, an entirely different and not very desirable result. Charles Bennett, the messenger who carried the petition to Monterey at the beginning of

March, found the burdensome secret just as unbearable as Mrs. Wimmer or Jacob Wittmer. All the way down to the capital he left in his wake groups of people talking about Sutter's gold mine, some thrilled and excited but most of them indifferent or incredulous. There were people who were inclined to believe the whole thing was nothing but a hoax of the cunning Swiss, who deliberately spread the rumor to entice settlers to the Sacramento Valley. The *Star* and the *Californian*, the two newspapers in San Francisco (as Yerba Buena was now called) reported the fact of the discovery; but they considered it beneath their dignity to add any editorial comment outside of a few disparaging remarks for the optimists. Dr. Robert Semple, the lanky Kentuckian who tried in vain to make Benicia a successful rival of the City by the Golden Gate, would give more for a good coal mine than "for all the gold mines in the universe," and Vallejo, rather disinterestedly, wished his old opponent all kinds of good luck in the exploitation of the discovery.

The failure of obtaining a legal title did not

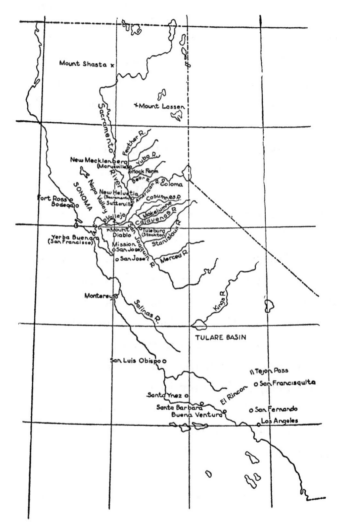

Mount Shasta x

+Mount Lassen

Sacramento River

Feather R.

New Mecklenberg
(Marysville)
Hock Farm
Yuba R.

Bear R.

Coloma
American R.

New Helvetia
(Sacramento)
Sutterville

Cosumnes R.

SONOMA

Napa Valley

Fort Ross
Bodega

Vallejo

Mokelumne

Calaveras R.

Mount
Diablo
Tuleburg
(Stockton)

Stanislaus R.

Yerba Buena
(San Francisco)

Mission
San Jose

o San Jose?

Merced R.

Monterey

Salinas R.

Kings R.

TULARE BASIN

San Luis Obispo o

ll Tejon Pass

o San Francisquita

Santa Ynez o

El Rincon

o San Fernando

Santa Barbara
Buena Ventura

Los Angeles

o

CALIFORNIA IN SUTTER'S TIME

[206]

deter Sutter from going ahead with his plans. After an experienced Georgian miner, Isaac Humphry, was conveniently discovered in San Francisco, Sutter formed with Marshall and Wimmer a mining company to exploit the gold deposits along the American River. Sutter's alleged premonitions, of which he talks so often, were the results of bitter experiences later on, and his complaints about early difficulties have really no foundation. As late as the twelfth of May he had enough laborers to undertake such an unimportant task as whitewashing the walls of the Fort. Indeed, it appeared at first that the principals of the lucky strike would really be able to enjoy the profits of their discovery.

Unfortunately there lived near the Fort a man who may be rightly called Sutter's evil spirit, Samuel Brannan. The *New Helvetia Diary* reveals that he went to the gold mines on Thursday, May fourth, returned after two days, and left quietly for San Francisco on the following Monday. A few days later a man ran through the streets of San Francisco, swinging his sombrero in one hand

and a bottle of gold dust in the other and shouting at the top of his voice: "Gold! Gold! Gold from the American River!" He was none other than the owner of the "shirt-tail store," advancing his interests by a subtle method which suspicious persons had attributed to Sutter himself. These shouts seemed at last to have made the people of California realize that digging for gold was more than just a fad. Within a few weeks the country went crazy. The last entries in the *New Helvetia Diary* record that the stream of gold-greedy humanity had begun to flow past Sutter's Fort into the mountains of California.

After the twenty-fifth of May the diary at the Fort was discontinued. The difficulties had apparently begun.

'After the discovery of gold was known, it began 'to spread like wild-fire all over California and 'then all over the world. With that, all my plans 'and projects came to naught. One after another 'of my people disappeared in the direction of the 'gold fields. Only the Mormons behaved decently at 'first. They were sorry for the difficulties in which

'I found myself, and some of them remained to fin-
'ish their jobs. But in the long run, they too could
'not resist the temptation. The first party of Mor-
'mons left for Coloma as early as March seventh,
'and the rest of them followed later. Only the sick
'and the crippled remained behind. Since I could
'not leave the Fort, I became a partner of a gold
'digging company which Wimmer and Marshall, to-
'gether with an experienced miner by the name of
'Isaac Humphry, had formed in the beginning of
'April at Coloma. I furnished the company with
'Indians, teams, and provisions, but I soon found
'that I was losing money and gave up the under-
'taking. Some of my neighbors, who were struck
'by the gold fever and went to the mountains pros-
'pecting, were more successful than I.

'The damage which I suffered in 1848 is in-
'estimable. In my tannery, which had developed
'into a very extensive and profitable business, the
'vats were left filled and a large quantity of half-
'finished leather was spoiled together with a large
'stock of raw hides, which had been left over from
'my last killing, or which I had bought from farm-

'ers. The same thing happened in every other
'branch of industry that I was carrying on at that
'time. The shoe and the saddle, the hat and the
'blacksmith shops were instantly deserted and the
'work left half-completed. As a great favor one of
'the blacksmiths remained a few days to repair
'some wagons. While everybody else was digging
'and washing gold, I tried to harvest my wheat
'crop. With the help of the Indians, I saved at
'least part of it. Two-thirds of the harvest, to be
'sure, had to be left in the fields.

'Finally, even the Indians had no more patience
'to work alone in harvesting and threshing my
'wheat crop. Other Indians, engaged by white men
'to work for them, had quantities of gold for which
'they bought all kinds of articles in the stores at
'enormous prices. When my Indians saw this, they
'too wished to go to the mountains to dig for the all
'powerful metal. At last I consented. I got a num-
'ber of wagons ready, loaded them with provisions
'and goods of all kinds, appointed a caretaker, and
'left with about one hundred Indians and a large
'number of Sandwich Islanders. The first camp

'was about ten miles above Mormon Island on the
'south fork of the American River. In a few weeks
'the place was so crowded with other miners that it
'did not pay any longer. I broke up the camp and
'started on the march further south. We located
'this time at Sutter Creek, now in Amador County,
'where I thought we should be alone. The work was
'going on well for a while until three or four
'traveling grog-shops were established within one
'and a half or two miles from the camp. Then, of
'course, the gold was taken to these places and
'spent in drinking and gambling, and the follow-
'ing day the men were sick and unable to work.
'My laborers, especially the Kanakas, became more
'and more indebted to me, and I found that it was
'high time to quit this sort of business in which I
'only lost time and money. I therefore broke up
'this camp too, and returned to the Fort where I
'disbanded nearly all the people who had worked
'for me in the mountains digging gold. The whole
'expedition proved to be a heavy loss to me.

'Another attempt to profit by the gold rush like-
'wise turned into a failure. I opened a business at

'Coloma with Lansford Hastings. But Hastings
'was unworthy of my trust. The business made
'good profits, but I lost money.

'During March and April only small parties of
'curious people from San Francisco passed the
'Fort on their way to the gold fields. The big rush
'did not set in until the middle of May; then the
'whole country seemed to have gone mad. Mer-
'chants, physicians, lawyers, sea captains left their
'wives and families in San Francisco in order to
'become gold diggers. Soldiers deserted their flag
'and sailors left their ships to rot in the harbor.
'The recently opened school had to be closed.
'Teacher and pupils had gone off to the mines.
'Everything was in confusion and most people did
'not know what to do. They offered their houses
'and lots in San Francisco for a few hundred dol-
'lars—lots which are now worth a hundred thou-
'sand dollars or more. The clever fellows did not
'stay in the gold fields, but returned immediately
'to San Francisco to buy up everything that they
'could lay hands on. Very soon vessels came to the
'port with all kinds of merchandise, and all the old

SUTTER AS MAJOR GENERAL

Painting in the Capitol at Sacramento

SUTTER IN HIS LATER LIFE

SUTTER'S LAST RESTING PLACE

'trash which had been lying for years unsold in 'the harbors of South and Central America, of 'Mexico, and of the Sandwich Islands found a 'profitable market in California.

'Toward the end of May Samuel Kyburz es-'tablished a hotel in the large building of the Fort 'and made a great deal of money. Many traders 'deposited their goods in my store, which was in 'charge of a trustworthy Indian. Soon, however, 'every little shanty in or around the Fort became 'a store, a warehouse, or a hotel; the whole settle-'ment was a veritable bazaar. My ferry could 'hardly take care of all the people who crossed the 'river every day. Since every white person con-'sidered it beneath his dignity to work at that time, 'a number of Indians attended to the ferry boat. 'Being more honest than most white people, every 'evening they delivered the money that they had 'taken in, deducting only the price for a few bot-'tles of brandy.

'The Fourth of July, 1848, I celebrated with a 'great banquet to which all the prominent men of 'the neighborhood were invited. Governor Richard

'Mason, Captain William Sherman, and Captain
'Joseph Folsom stopped on the eve of the celebra-
'tion at my Fort, while on a tour of inspection
'through northern California and the gold dis-
'tricts. The escort which had accompanied them
'into the mountains had, as was to be expected, de-
'serted them. I invited the officers to rest over the
'Fourth of July and to join with me in its celebra-
'tion.

'The day began with the hoisting of the flags
'and the firing of the cannon. It was a universal
'holiday, and being the first national holiday to be
'celebrated under the American flag, everybody
'was in high spirits. All rejoiced in being under
'a good and strong government now. The table
'was set in my old armory hall and Kyburz, with
'the help of a number of women who were at the
'Fort at that time, had prepared an excellent din-
'ner. We had beef, game, and fowl, and all the
'luxuries which a frontier life could offer. A
'French captain had just brought up in his launch
'a supply of good sauterne, brandy, and other
'drinks. Toasts were proposed and healths were

'drunk. "Philosopher" Charles Pickett was the
'orator of the day. All ate and drank freely, and
'soon general hilarity prevailed. General Sherman
'says in his memoirs that I was "tight" that day,
'but I was no more intoxicated than he. Men can-
'not drink liquor without feeling the effects of it.
'I believe it was bad taste for an officer of the army
'to partake of my hospitality and then make flip-
'pant remarks about it, accusing the host of
'drunkenness. I think that Sherman was later
'ashamed of his words; in a letter, which he wrote
'to me, he took back everything and begged my
'pardon.'

XIII
The Aftermath

WHEN the first national holiday after the signing of the treaty of Guadalupe Hidalgo, February second, 1848, was celebrated, the founder of New Helvetia had no cause to despair. To be sure, most of the grain was rotting on the fields and the mills and shops stood almost still; a skilled mechanic had to be paid ten dollars a day and ordinary white laborers could often not be had for less than one dollar an hour. But every nook and corner of the buildings was rented at a high price: Kyburz paid a monthly rent of five hundred dollars for the "big house," and single rooms brought as much as one hundred dollars. Horses and cattle sold at five times their former value, schooner and ferry brought handsome profits, the store did a flourishing business, and the value of Sutter's vast holdings of real estate was sure to rise to staggering amounts. Sherman, who, by the way, modified his "flippant remarks" in the later editions of his *Memoirs*, estimated the cost of the aforesaid dinner on the Fourth of July at fifteen hundred to two thousand dollars. He received such a favorable impression of Sutter's position that he wrote a few weeks later: "This man Sutter has played a conspicuous part in the history of this country, and is likely to continue his onward career."

Unfortunately, just at this critical time of the settlement's transition from a manorial estate to a business center, the Russian-American Company became tired of waiting for the balance of the purchasing price which Sutter still owed them. Probably believing that Sutter wallowed in gold now, they threatened to attach New Helvetia. In order to save himself and his other creditors from the impending catastrophe, he followed the advice

of his associates, and in October 1848 he signed
over his property to his oldest son who had arrived
from Switzerland just a few weeks before. John
Augustus, the younger, appointed Peter Burnett,
later governor, his agent, and during Sutter's absence the two started the city of Sacramento by
offering lots for sale around the Fort and at the
embarcadero. It was done against the express desire
of Sutter who had intended the town of Sutterville, laid out by Bidwell and Hastings in January
1846, for the metropolis of the valley. But the
money realized from the sales enabled Sutter to
pay off all his old debts within a few months and
to commission one of his trusted servants, Friedrich Lienhard, who in later years wrote a rather
unflattering account of his dealings with Sutter,
to conduct the rest of his family to California. In
March 1849, Sutter rented out the Fort and transferred the movable property and the live stock to
the Hock-Farm on the Feather River.

At about the same time the conquest of the
Sacramento Valley by the gold-seekers began. On
the last day of February, the *California* emptied

the first load of argonauts in the harbor of San Francisco, and from then on ever-increasing hordes from the United States and from Europe, from South America and from Australia, were let loose upon California. A man less generous, less trusting, and less careless in his business dealings might even now have been able to cope with the new situation and to have salvaged at least a portion of his fortune, but Sutter was trampled under the feet of the marching columns of gold-hungry regiments and his holdings melted away like snow in the sun. He continued to sell parcels of his land but the better part of the profits flowed into the pockets of unscrupulous agents, and every dollar which he did receive he needed to pay the lawyers who presented his case before the land commission and the courts. For in the meantime squatters had begun to settle upon his lands, denying Sutter's title to the property. After their armed uprising was speedily suppressed by the law-abiding citizens of Sacramento, they organized and contested every step of Sutter's efforts to have his Mexican land grants confirmed by the United States.

'During the winter of 1848-49, while I was
'snowed in in the mountains, the city of Sacra-
'mento was laid out by the landing place at the
'river. To my son, John A. Sutter, Junior, who had
'arrived from Switzerland before the rest of my
'family came, I had given power of attorney, and
'it was easy for Sam Brannan to win my son over
'to his favorite project of a city near the Fort.

'I had always been opposed to the plan of estab-
'lishing the metropolis of the valley at New Hel-
'vetia. The location was favorable enough, to be
'sure, but the land was so low that a rise of the
'river above normal would cause a flood in the
'town. This contention was proven in later years
'by repeated floods with heavy loss of life and
'property. For this very reason, I had started the
'city of Sutterville several years before the gold
'discovery. Sutterville was located about three
'miles below the Fort on rising ground, high above
'the level of the river. From Sutterville a high and
'dry wagon road to the mountains could easily
'have been built. The town prospered from its very
'start. A number of stores and houses were built

'immediately, and several vessels anchored regu-
'larly at the landing place. Doctor George Mc-
'Kinstry, Theodor Cordua, and many others were
'interested in the new settlement. John McDougal,
'later governor of California, and his brother had
'a store-ship at Sutterville from which they sold
'goods. There lay at anchor in the river five or six
'other ships, whose owners intended to build stores.
'It was in Sutterville that the first brick house
'in the Sacramento Valley was erected in 1846 by
'the Alsatian, George Zinns, who, in the following
'year, married Mrs. Wolfinger, one of the sur-
'vivors of the Donner Party.

'Now Sam Brannan, who had moved his store
'from the Fort to the waterfront, and other mer-
'chants at New Helvetia, as Barton Lee and Pierre
'Cornwall, wanted to have the town near the Fort.
'They knew that the merchants at Sutterville were
'their rivals, and it was really jealousy which built
'the city of Sacramento. This would never have
'happened, had I not been snow-bound at Coloma.
'As matters stood, I could do nothing else but
'agree to everything, even to the name of Sacra-

'mento, which my son and Brannan had selected.

'At that time the land around the Fort still
'belonged to me. I had sold a number of lots and
'given others away gratis. My son had appointed
'as his agent the future governor, Peter Burnett,
'who made a fortune much too quickly to suit me.
'Neither did I like my son's management of the
'affairs and so I revoked my power of attorney
'which he held. I commissioned other agents to
'place on the market the unsold lots of Sacramento,
'agreeing to let them have a rather high percent-
'age of the profit. However, my choice too did not
'prove to be a fortunate one. One of them made
'a fortune out of me in a very short time. As my
'agent he earned some eighty thousand dollars,
'which formed a handsome corner stone for the
'city block he built later. The next agent sold a
'great many lots but never accounted for them.
'Besides this he borrowed five thousand dollars on
'my account at ten per cent interest a month. He
'did not tell me a word about it and in 1856, the
'debt amounted to thirty-five thousand dollars.
'While I was resting peacefully with my family at

'Hock-Farm, not knowing that I owed a dollar 'in the world, the sheriff made his appearance and 'attached my property. I was obliged to go to the 'county seat at Nicolaus and pay a note for thirty 'thousand dollars.

'In this manner my large holdings disappeared. 'I was the victim of every swindler who came along. 'I understood little about business and was foolish 'enough to have faith in men who cheated me on 'every side. Before the discovery of gold I had 'honest men around me like Bidwell, Hensley, 'Reading, etc. These had inspired me with confi-'dence in human nature and caused me to trust 'many a sharper who was swept into California 'on the wave of the gold excitement.

'My grist mill was never finished. Everything 'was stolen, even the stones. There is an old saying 'that a man will steal everything but a mile stone 'and a mill stone, but my mill stones actually were 'stolen. The miners would not buy anything that 'they could more easily steal. They stole the cattle 'and the horses, they stole the bells from the Fort 'and the weights from the gates, they stole the

'hides, and they stole the barrels. I had just made
'two hundred barrels for salmon which I had begun
'to cure at that time. I had tried it out carefully
'and had ascertained that it would be a very good
'business. All the barrels were stolen, of course.
'Even the cannon which I had not yet given away
'to my neighbors were carried off. My property
'was entirely exposed and at the mercy of the
'rabble. I could not shut the gates of my Fort in
'order to keep them out; they would have broken
'them down. The country swarmed with lawless
'men. Immigrants drove their stock into my yard
'and wasted my grain. Talking to them did not do
'any good. I was alone and there was no law. Any
'one who felt offended pulled out his revolver. One
'man was shot for a slight provocation in the Fort,
'right under my very nose.

'In March 1849 I moved to my Hock-Farm
'which had been laid out in 1842. Bidwell had
'built a fine mansion for me there and had pre-
'pared everything for the reception of my family,
'whose arrival from Switzerland I was expecting
'just then.

The Aftermath

'My live stock continued to be decreased by kill-
'ing and stealing. It soon turned out that trans-
'ferring the animals to Hock-Farm had not
'improved the situation and numerous horses were
'stolen and entire *manadas* of mares were driven
'to Oregon. The few *vaqueros* who remained in my
'service were not strong enough to prevent the
'wholesale thefts. My large stock of hogs was like-
'wise an easy prey for the robbers. One day a man
'by the name of Owens from Missouri proposed to
'me that I let him kill all the cattle which had
'strayed beyond the Buttes. I agreed to this sug-
'gestion with the understanding that I should re-
'ceive half of the profits. I knew that the people
'from Marysville would kill off these cattle any-
'way. Mr. Owens started his work by slaughtering
'a fine Durham cow which had cost me three hun-
'dred dollars, and I had to chase him away.

'During the great flood of 1849, the cattle had
'to take refuge on the islands and knolls between
'the Buttes and the mouth of the Feather River.
'Here my *vaqueros* could not guard them at all
'and people from the surrounding towns ap-

'proached by boat and killed hundreds of animals.
'During the winter of 1849-50, five men formed a
'partnership for the purpose of slaughtering my
'cattle. They hired a number of people and a boat's
'crew and actually monopolized the meat market
'at Sacramento. In the spring these men divided
'a profit of sixty thousand dollars among them-
'selves and left for the Atlantic coast. Some of
'these fellows returned the following year, hired a
'number of men and started the business all over
'again. Fortunately law and order had, to a certain
'extent, been restored in the country. When my
'*vaqueros* found these men killing some of my
'cows, I sent immediately to Nicolaus for the
'sheriff. This sheriff, an old man from New York
'by the name of J. Hopkins, demanded a strong
'posse. When the robbers saw our people approach,
'they became frightened and jumped into their
'boats, disregarding the sheriff's demand for sur-
'render. Since the latter would not allow my men
'to fire at the boats, the cattle thieves made their
'escape.

'Marshall became very poor after the discovery

'of gold. He always had great projects in his head.
'Following the guidance of his spirit, he flitted
'hither and thither about the foothills. Once he
'asked me for help and I gave him one or two
'horses and a few Indians. But they returned after
'several weeks very much disgusted and said that
'they would not go with him any more. Neverthe-
'less, I fitted him out again when he came back and
'asked me for more men and horses. All his efforts
'were in vain, and he never succeeded in striking
'it as richly as he hoped. The curse of the gold
'seemed to last on him.

'On the third of September, 1849, the constitu-
'tional convention met at Monterey. I was elected
'delegate from Sacramento. On the way to Mon-
'terey I caught a fever, but fortunately I recovered
'after a few days. As usual I stopped at David
'Spence's house where Abel Stearns was also a
'guest. We worked very hard at this convention.
'We compared the constitutions of the various
'states and selected what was best suited for our
'conditions. When the question of slavery came up,
'the people from the southern states kept quiet;

'they did not wish to be excluded from the distri-
'bution of offices. We held many night sessions, and
'in six weeks the whole business was done—to the
'chagrin of those who had nothing else to do and
'wanted to spin it out as long as they could. The
'last day of the convention, our president, Doctor
'Robert Semple, was sick and I was elected presi-
'dent. That day we went in a body to General
'Bennett Riley, the last of the military governors
'of California, in order to inform him of the con-
'clusion of our work. Preceded by the sergeant-at-
'arms, I led a procession with Senator William
'Gwin on one arm and Delegate M. M. McCarver
'on the other, followed by all the other members
'of the convention, as well as all the secretaries and
'clerks. I delivered an address to the Governor,
'thanking him for his assistance. In his reply Gen-
'eral Riley remarked that next to the day of the
'battle of Contraros, this was the happiest day of
'his life. Then he had wine served of which he had
'a rich supply and many toasts were drunk. After
'this the ambulances were ready to take most of
'us up to San Jose. Major, afterwards General,

'E. Canby was in charge of these wagons, which
'were hardly ever used in California, and loaned
'them to us for this occasion.

'While we were in San Jose, my friends wanted
'to make me a candidate for governor. I declined
'at that time, and when I finally accepted, it was
'too late. P. H. Burnett had stumped the state
'and beat me, notwithstanding the fact that San
'Francisco alone gave me a thousand votes. Bur-
'nett had been in the mountains several days ahead
'of me, otherwise he would never have defeated me.
'Burnett resigned after one year and J. McDougal
'took his place. The legislature, which was elected
'at the same time, contained only about one-third
'good and honest men. Of the rest, many appeared
'in the legislative halls with revolvers and bowie-
'knives fastened to their belts. They were drinking,
'rioting, and swearing nearly all the time.

'In January 1852 the land commission, which
'was appointed by the U. S. Government to settle
'the various land claims, opened its sessions in San
'Francisco. The State as well as the Federal Gov-
'ernment were at fault in passing on land claims;

[229]

'they favored the squatters altogether too much.
'However, my two land grants were finally con-
'firmed by the commission in 1857, and in the
'following year this decision was upheld by the
'U. S. District Court for the Northern District of
'California. A whole steamboat load of my friends
'came to Hock-Farm to congratulate me.

'The squatters then appealed to the Supreme
'Court at Washington. Their attorney had ad-
'vantage with the judges and succeeded in con-
'vincing them that there was a flaw in my second
'title. So the Court decided against me. My first
'grant, to be sure, was confirmed again, but the
'so-called *sobrante* grant was declared void because
'Micheltorena had signed the deed in camp at El
'Rincon and not at the capital. Since I had given
'away many titles from Micheltorena's grant I was
'now obliged to make these good, and in this man-
'ner I lost all my estates. The annual three thou-
'sand dollars, which the California legislature had
'voted for ten years, was not a gift of the State to
'me nor would I have accepted it as such. This
'amount was only a return of the taxes which I

'had paid on the *sobrante* land grant, later taken
'away from me.

'When I started building my sawmill at Coloma,
'some smart merchants in San Francisco called
'this another folly of Sutter's. Well, this folly was
'the indirect cause of the State developing into a
'prosperous country within a few years, of helping
'thousands and thousands of people to fortunes,
'and of saving the world from financial bank-
'ruptcy after the crisis of 1849-50. As far as my
'own fate is concerned, to be sure, it was the great-
'est folly which I ever committed. Without the
'discovery of gold, I would now be the richest man
'on the shores of the Pacific.

'For eleven years I have been a petitioner before
'Congress pleading for justice. The *sobrante* grant
'at one dollar and twenty-five cents an acre, just
'what the government received for it, would
'amount to one hundred twenty-two thousand dol-
'lars. This is the sum for which I am asking. The
'members of the committee were afraid to ask for
'the whole amount and proposed a recompense of
'fifty thousand dollars. I am sure that I will receive

'this sum, though in order to get it, I have already
'spent twenty-five thousand dollars and owe to my
'lawyers an additional ten thousand dollars.

'Such is the irony of fate.'

XIV

Disappointment and Death

WHEN on the thirteenth of October, 1849, thirty-
one guns of the fort of Monterey announced the
adoption of the constitution and the end of the
constituent assembly, the curtain fell for John
Augustus Sutter's brief but brilliant performance
as an historical character. The following third
period of his life, almost equal in length to the period which preceded the dramatic decade from
1839 to 1849, was taken up by a bitter and dis-
appointing struggle to retrieve at least a fraction
of his fortune. During this struggle the walls of
Fort Sutter crumbled, and his name gradually

lost its magic. In the summer of 1880 few people outside of California took notice of his death, and in 1925 his name was so completely forgotten by the world at large that Blaise Cendrars' shilling shocker could pass as a biography of the great pioneer.

To be sure, in the annals of the State his name is mentioned again and again during the following years. Too many had been befriended by the generous Swiss, too important had been his activities that his name could be so easily forgotten. On the sixteenth of February, 1853, the rank of major-general was conferred upon him by the legislature of California, and two years later the capitol in Sacramento was adorned with his life-size portrait. Every year when San Francisco celebrated the admission of California into the Union or when Sacramento paraded on the Fourth of July under the auspices of the "Ancient and Independent Order of 'Bricks,'" the venerable General, at the head of the "Sutter Rifles" or surrounded by his staff, rode proudly in the parade. On Admission Day, September tenth, 1855, Hon. George Johnston gave voice to the esteem in which Sutter stood, when he concluded his oration at the American Theater in San Francisco with these words: "Especially let us dwell with admiration upon the history of one of the oldest and most notable of that band—pure in heart—dispensing his hospitality with the prodigality of God's gift to men —comforting the wayworn and weary immigrants —ministering to the wants of the dying—bestowing the last words of respect upon the dead—once the owner of a princely domain—in his old age harassed and beset by pecuniary and other worldly difficulties: always, however, through every change, in every phase of varied fortune, the same lofty, stainless, and genial nature: let us regard the venerable Sutter as a model worthy of our imitation, an object deserving our sincerest esteem."

Proudly as Sutter may have listened to such high praise, it could hardly recompense him for the blow which the aftermath of the gold discovery had dealt him. His original property was overrun by squatters or passed out of his hands, partly through his own fault, partly through the manipulations of unscrupulous agents and lawyers; only with difficulty could he prevent his beautiful Hock-Farm from being sold under the hammer. His last hope was destroyed when in December 1864, the United States Supreme Court reversed the decision of the District Court in regard to the *sobrante* grant by Micheltorena. More than once he intended to leave the State and settle in Europe or on the Hawaiian Islands. But not until a fiendish act robbed him of his home on the Feather River did he leave the country to which he was attached with every fiber of his body. A terse account in the *Marysville Weekly Appeal* of the twenty-second of June, 1865, reports with dramatic clarity the final misfortune of the pioneer: "The old residence of General Sutter at the Hock-Farm was destroyed by fire Wednesday morning, June twenty-first. The fire also extended to a barley field. The house was completely destroyed— home, clothing, pictures, busts, curiosities and everything he had been accumulating for the last forty years, except a few medals and his family

portraits. A large library owned by the general
was also destroyed. The fire was the work of an
incendiary—supposed to be a discharged soldier,
who had been hanging about the premises the past
few days, and who had been caught stealing and
punished by being tied up. There was no insur-
ance."

A few months later, Sutter visited for the last
time the cities and towns which had grown up on
his old domain. On the sixth of October, Governor
Frederick F. Lowe handed him a letter of introduction to the Senate and the House of Representatives with a strong recommendation to
consider Sutter's claim for indemnity for services
rendered to the nation and for losses sustained as
a result of the discovery of gold. A little later he
left for Washington, D. C., where he resided till
1871, when he moved to Lititz in Pennsylvania, a
little town founded by the Moravian Brethren in
1756. He built himself a comfortable house and
spent the rest of his days as a respected burgher.

A pleasing picture of the aging pioneer is given
by Hubert Howe Bancroft who went to Lititz in

the fall of 1876 to write down Sutter's reminiscences:

"After knocking loudly at the portal several times, the door was slowly, silently opened a little way, and the head of an old woman appeared at the aperture.

" 'Is this Mrs. Sutter?' I asked.

"No response.

" 'May I speak with you a moment in the hall?'

"Still no response, and no encouragement for me to enter. There she stood, the guardian of apparently as impregnable a fortress as ever was Fort Sutter in its palmiest days. I must gain admission; retreat now might be fatal. Stepping toward the small opening as if there was no obstacle whatever to my entering, and as the door swung back a little at my approach, I slipped into the hall.

"Once within, no ogress was there. Mrs. Sutter was a tall, thin, intelligent Swiss, plainly dressed, and having a shawl thrown over her shoulders. Her English was scarcely intelligible, but she easily understood me, and her deafness was not at all troublesome.

"Handing her my card, I asked to see General Sutter. 'I know he is ill,' said I, 'but I must see him.' Taking the card, she showed me into a back parlor and then withdrew. From Mrs. Sutter's manner, no less than from what had been told me at the hotel, I was extremely fearful that I had come too late, and that all of the history that house contained was in the fevered brain of a dying man.

"But presently, to my great astonishment and delight, the door opened, and the General himself entered at a brisk pace. He appeared neither very old nor very feeble. The chance for a history of Sutter's Fort was improving. He was rather below medium height and stout. His step was still firm, his bearing soldierly, and in his younger days he must have been a man of much endurance, with a remarkably fine physique. His features were of the German cast, broad, full face, fairly intellectual forehead, with white hair, bald on the top of the head, white side whiskers, mustache, and imperial;

a deep, clear, earnest eye met yours truthfully. Seventy-five years, apparently, sat upon him not heavily. He was suffering severely from rheumatism, and he used a cane to assist him in walking about the house. He complained of failing memory, but I saw no indication of it in the five days dictating which followed.

"No one could be in General Sutter's presence long without feeling satisfied that, if not of the shrewdest, he was an inborn gentleman. He had more the manners of a courtier than those of a backwoodsman, with this difference: his speech and bearing were the promptings of a kind heart, unaffected and sincere. He received me courteously, and listened with deep attention to my plan for a history of the Pacific States."

The claim for indemnity, of which Sutter speaks in the last chapter of his memoirs, was submitted to Congress in 1866. Although the bill was renewed by his friends in every session, Sutter did not even receive the fifty thousand dollars of which he had been so sure when he dictated his reminiscences. In 1880 the claim came before the House

for the sixteenth time, but Congress adjourned
on the sixteenth of June without having taken
action. Two days later the great pioneer died at
Mades' Hotel in Washington, D. C. A close friend
of his later years, Colonel Frank Schaeffer, was at
his bedside; a sad letter to his wife lay half finished
on his table.

On the twenty-fourth of June, the *Associated
Pioneers of the Territorial Days of California* conducted him, their president since 1878, to his final
resting place. General H. G. Gibson, the acting
president, delivered the eulogy. General Frémont,
who at the time of the Mexican War had exchanged bitter words with Sutter, used touching
expressions of praise in parting from his "friend,
companion, and associate." His remains rest in
the cemetery of the Moravians in Lititz beside
those of his wife, who followed him in death on the
nineteenth of January, 1881.

Thirty years later the people of California
erected a fitting monument to the "pioneer of
pioneers" by restoring the Fort to its original
state.

Author's Note

This book attempts to tell without fictitious embellishments the story of the most colorful character in Pacific Coast history. The "reminiscences" of Sutter, which form the major part of the narrative, were dictated to the historian H. H. Bancroft in the fall of 1876. A publication of the original would have not even academic interest; it presents only in a very limited sense Sutter's own words. Therefore, I have rewritten the entire story, correcting the numerous errors, inserting the necessary dates and names, supplying connecting passages wherever advisable, and arranging it in chronological order as far as possible. In cases where Sutter's story forms a connected narrative, especially where it rises to a dramatic climax, I have endeavored to retain his own words as much as possible. Needless to say, I considered it my duty not to alter those passages where the pioneer gives his prejudiced version of certain events, consciously exaggerating or distorting the facts. As far as it appeared necessary to correct Sutter's statements in the light of historical truth, it has been done in my interpolations. The names of some men whom Sutter accuses of having cheated him have been omitted. In most cases it is impossible to verify these charges and they are of no historical importance. The large gaps in the "reminiscences" I have filled with passages from Sutter's so-called "diary," written in the spring of 1856, from the *New Helvetia Diary*, which was kept at Fort Sutter from 1845 to 1848, from the article which the general wrote for *Hutching's California Magazine* in 1857, and in a few cases from his letters. Where interpolations were necessary to complete and clarify the picture, I have continued the story from my own notes, the results of many happy hours of research among the treasures of the Bancroft Library of the University of California. The recent investigations of Dr. J. P. Zollinger, R. Bigler, and myself have enabled me to give a correct version of Sutter's years before his coming to America. Julian Dana in his sympathetic biography, *Sutter of California,* gives a more detailed account of Sutter and his family; his interpretation of the historical character, however, differs essentially from mine.

To Herbert E. Bolton, my teacher and friend, I wish to dedicate this modest contribution to the history of our beautiful State.

Erwin G. Gudde.

University of California, April sixth, 1936.